THE PAULINE CIRCLE

OTHER WORKS BY F. F. BRUCE

The Epistle to the Galatians: A Commentary on the Greek Text

The Spreading Flame
Israel and the Nations
Second Thoughts on the Dead Sea Scrolls
An Expanded Paraphrase of the Epistles of Paul
This is That
Tradition Old and New
Answers to Questions
The Message of the New Testament
Paul: Apostle of the Free Spirit
The Time is Fulfilled
Men and Movements in the Primitive Church

THE PAULINE CIRCLE

F. F. Bruce

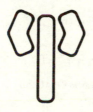

WILLIAM B. EERDMANS PUBLISHING COMPANY

THE PATERNOSTER PRESS

British Library Cataloguing in Publication Data

Bruce, F.F.
  The Pauline circle.
  1. Paul, The Apostle, Saint   2. Christian
saints——Turkey——Tarsus——Biography
  3. Tarsus (Turkey)——Biography
  I. Title
  226'.6'0924   BS2506
  ISBN 0-85364-397-0

Library of Congress Cataloging in Publication Data
Bruce, F. F. (Frederick Fyvie), 1910–
  The Pauline circle.

  Includes index.
  1. Paul, the Apostle, Saint—Friends and associates.
I. Title.
BS2506.B756 1984   225.9'22 [B]   84–26027
ISBN 0-8028-0066-1

*Photoset in Great Britain by
Photo·Graphics Ltd, Honiton, Devon.
and printed for the Paternoster Press.
Paternoster House, 3 Mount Radford Crescent, Exeter, Devon, and
William B. Eerdmans Publishing Company,
255 Jefferson Ave., S.E., Grand Rapids, Mich. 49503, U.S.A.
by A. Wheaton & Co., Ltd., Exeter, U.K.*

Contents

Preface   7

Introduction   8

1. Ananias and the disciples at Damascus   11

2. Barnabas, the Levite from Cyprus   15

3. Silas/Silvanus   23

4. Timothy of Lystra   29

5. Luke, the beloved physician   35

6. Priscilla and Aquila   44

7. Apollos of Alexandria   51

8. Titus of Antioch   58

9. Onesimus of Colossae   66

10. Mark, the cousin of Barnabas   73

11. Paul's co-workers   81

12. Hosts and hostesses   91

Index   103

To

JEREMY AND MARGARET MUDDITT

Preface

The twelve chapters in this little book appeared originally in successive issues of *The Harvester*, in the section 'Exploring the Bible', throughout the year 1983. I am grateful to the publishers and editors, and especially to the sectional editor, Mr. John Polkinghorne, for giving them house-room in that form, and now I am grateful to The Paternoster Press for publishing them in this form.

F. F. B.

Introduction

On the bookshelf which accommodates works on the
Fourth Gospel may be seen such titles as *The Johannine
Circle,*[1] *The Johannine School,*[2] and *The Community of the
Beloved Disciple.*[3] These are devoted to the associates or
disciples who are believed to have gathered round
John the Evangelist, especially after his migration to
Ephesus. But to give an account of these people calls
for a fair degree of imaginative reconstruction – a task,
nevertheless, well worth undertaking.

If, however, we think of the Pauline circle, the
evidence for its membership lies plentifully before us in
the New Testament, both in Paul's own writings and
in the Acts. Paul attracted friends around him as a
magnet attracts iron filings. His genius for friendship

[1] By O. Cullmann (SCM Press, 1975).
[2] By R.A. Culpepper (Scholars Press, Missoula, 1975).
[3] By R.E. Brown (Geoffrey Chapman, 1979).

has been spoken of so often that it has become proverbial – almost a cliché, in fact. There are about seventy people mentioned by name in the New Testament of whom we should never have heard were it not for their association with Paul, and over and above these there is a host of unnamed friends. He appears to have had the gift, moreover, of readily winning the friendship of non-Christians, like the Asiarchs[4] in Ephesus (Acts 19:31) and the centurion Julius (Acts 27:3, 43).[5] Although he was nothing much to look at, he plainly had that warm and outgoing kind of personality which draws out people's good will and affection. The other side of the coin is shown by those who could not stand him at any price: people were rarely neutral towards him.

Our primary source of information about Paul's friends and associates is, naturally, his own letters. All the letters that bear his name are laid under contribution here. However uncertain the life-setting of the Pastorals (1 and 2 Timothy and Titus) may be, their personal notes have a special interest, particularly where the persons mentioned are known to us from the other letters. Part of the special interest in the Pastoral notes on those people lies in trying to fit the references to them into their careers as otherwise known to us.

Our principal secondary source of information is Acts. Confidence in the trustworthiness of the references in Acts to members of Paul's circle is enhanced

[1] A body comprising leading citizens from the chief cities in the province of Asia. See p. 49.
[5] Even when one cannot speak of him as making friends, he appears (according to Luke) to have made a not unfavourable impression on many persons in positions of power - on the proconsuls Sergius Paullus and Gallio (Acts 13:7–12: 18:12–17), on Felix, procurator of Judaea, with his wife Drusilla (Acts 24:22–26), and on his successor Festus, together with Herod Agrippa II and his sister Berenice, the elder sister of Drusilla (Acts 24:27–26:32).

by the unforced way in which those references chime in with the references to the same people in Paul's letters. On another occasion I have argued for an affirmative answer to the question, 'Is the Paul of Acts the real Paul?'[6] Here I think evidence is made available for a similarly affirmative answer to the question, 'Is the Pauline circle of Acts the real Pauline circle?'

[6] *Bulletin of the John Rylands University Library of Manchester* 58 (1975–76), pp. 282–305.

1

Ananias and the Disciples at Damascus

Paul's first friend after his conversion was Ananias of Damascus, the first man to call Paul 'brother' in the Christian sense. Ananias was a friend in need if ever there was one. At one blow Paul had lost his former friends; his chances of making new ones might have been reckoned slender. Paul's companions who took him to the house of Judas in the 'street called Straight'[1] certainly lent a helping hand, but they had no idea what had happened to him. Ananias had to be specially encouraged by the Lord to go and visit Paul, and Paul in turn was made aware of Ananias's impending visit.

Ananias appears to have been a Jewish believer of Damascus, not one of the refugees from Judaea. He knew about Paul by hearsay, and did not like what he knew. His character is depicted by Paul in Acts 22:12:

[1] Acts 9:11. See p. 92.

he was 'a devout man according to the law, well spoken of by all the Jews who lived' in Damascus. We should like to know how he became a disciple (as he is called in Acts 9:10) and who it was that first brought the gospel to Damascus, but we cannot be sure.[2]

Ananias was surprised indeed to learn of the change that had come about in Paul. The Ethiopian could more readily change his skin, surely, or the leopard its spots, than the arch-persecutor become a follower of the Nazarene. But when he was assured that this miracle had really taken place, he was willing to lay aside all his misgivings and hard feelings, to make his way to the house of Judas in the street called Straight and greet the blinded guest in that house as 'Brother Saul'. As Ananias laid his hands on him he recovered his sight and was filled with the Holy Spirit. It is possible also that Ananias baptized Paul. According to Acts 22:16 he said to Paul, 'Rise and get yourself baptized';[3] according to Acts 9:18, Paul 'rose and was baptized'.[4] It is uncertain whether Paul's baptism was self-administered (as proselyte baptism was) or administered by someone else, and in the latter case whether it was administered by Ananias or not. As Paul himself was later to point out to the Corinthians, it is a matter of no importance by whom a believer is baptized; what is of supreme importance is into whose name one is baptized.[5] So far as Paul's baptism is concerned, we are left in no doubt on this last score; as he was baptized, he was to call on Jesus' name, invoking him as Lord (Acts 22:16).

[2] The question is discussed somewhat more fully in my *Paul: Apostle of the Free Spirit* (Paternoster, 1977), pp. 76–80

[3] Gk. *baptisai*, aorist imperative middle.

[4] Gk. *ebaptisthē*, aorist indicative passive.

[5] 1 Cor. 1:14–17.

But that was not the only service that Ananias rendered to Paul. He was sent to him as the messenger of the risen Lord. Paul himself claims to have received his commission as part of the 'revelation of Jesus Christ' which was granted him on the Damascus road (Gal. 1:12, 15f.). But some at least of the implications of that commission were spelt out to him in greater detail by Ananias. When then he insists in Gal. 1:11f. that he neither received nor learned his gospel from a human being, does he overlook the part that Ananias played? No. He is concerned there to refute the charge that his knowledge of the gospel and his commission to preach it came from those who were apostles before him. Ananias was not a bearer of special authority like theirs; he was but a private disciple, and whatever message he carried from the risen Lord to Paul came as directly to Paul from the Lord as the words he heard on the Damascus road. Whatever part of Paul's commission came to him through the lips of Ananias was received by him not from a mere human being but from the exalted Christ in heaven.

Having delivered his message, Ananias disappears from the story. Paul, on the other hand, moves more and more into the forefront of the scene. But if Ananias lived on to learn something of Paul's apostolic ministry, he had good reason to look back with satisfaction on the day when he helped to steady Paul's feet as he was about to take his first steps on the Christian road.

There were other disciples at Damascus alongside Ananias. It was with them that Paul spent his first days as a believer and first enjoyed Christian fellowship. What they made of this strange new convert who came to join them for a short time we may try to imagine. But the first company of people with whom one enjoys Christian fellowship is liable to leave a distinctive impression. It was with them that Paul first broke the memorial bread and first shared Bible study in the light of the coming of Christ. In the synagogues of Damascus, to which he had been sent with letters of extradition authorizing him to arrest and take back to Jerusalem those followers of Jesus who had fled from his hostile attentions at home, Paul soon made new enemies as he proclaimed that same Jesus to be the Son of God. But among those who had trembled at the news of his coming to Damascus he quickly found new friends. The time came when he had reason to be thankful for their friendship. When his enemies laid an ambush for him by the city gates, it was these new friends who let him down through the window of a house built on to the city wall so that he made a safe getaway.[6] We do not know if he ever returned to Damascus, but the city and the disciples who lived there retained a special place in his memory and affection.

---

[6] 2 Cor. 11:32 f.; Acts 9:23–25. Between his first arrival in Damascus and his secret escape from the city he had spent some time in the kingdom of the Nabataean Arabs, east and south of Damascus (Gal. 1:17), and his activity there aroused the hostility of the Nabataean authorities.

2

Barnabas, the Levite from Cyprus

It would have been a debatable point in the primitive
church whether Barnabas belonged to the Pauline
circle or (as some would have hotly contended) Paul
belonged rather to the circle of Barnabas. It would be
fruitless to discuss this question; the inclusion of
Barnabas in this series is justified by the fact that for
some years the two men were closely associated.

If Ananias proved himself a friend in need to Paul in
Damascus, Barnabas performed the same service for
him when he returned to Jerusalem as a believer. His
old associates would have none of him, and those who
would most naturally be his new associates were
suspicious of him. So far as they knew, he might well
be an *agent provocateur*. 'But Barnabas took him, and
brought him to the apostles' (Acts 9:27), and told them
how Paul had already given proof of the genuineness
of his conversion. This implies some prior knowledge

of Paul on the part of Barnabas; it also shows what confidence the apostles had in Barnabas.

Barnabas, in fact, is a man of whom nothing but good is reported: Luke sums up his character by saying, 'he was a good man' (Acts 11:24). He first appears as a generous donor of a piece of land, or at least of the price that he got for it, to the common pool set up by the Jerusalem church for the maintenance of its poorer members. If it be asked how a Levite came to have landed property, the answer may be that it was a burial plot which, like many another pious Jew, he had acquired in the neighbourhood of Jerusalem. It is on first introducing him into his narrative that Luke tells us that Barnabas, 'the son of encouragement', was the sobriquet given him by the apostles (his original name was Joseph). The aptness of the sobriquet is unmistakable: wherever Barnabas found people or situations requiring encouragement, he gave all the encouragement of which he was capable. Both Paul and the Jerusalem church leaders benefited greatly by his encouragement on the occasion when he brought them together.

Barnabas's next appearance brings him to Antioch. Some of the Hellenistic believers who had left Jerusalem during the persecution that broke out after Stephen's death[1] made their way north through the province of Syria until they reached its capital city, Antioch on the Orontes. In those days Antioch was the third largest city in the world (surpassed only by Rome and Alexandria). It had a large Jewish element in its population, and the Hellenists from Jerusalem, on their arrival, shared the gospel with their fellow-

---

[1] On Stephen see my *Men and Movements in the Primitive Church* (Paternoster, 1979), pp. 49–62.

Jews, as they had done in other places. But some more adventurous spirits among them, men from Cyprus and Cyrene, conceived the novel idea of trying the good news out on Gentiles, to see how they would react to it. The Gentiles' reaction was astonishing: they embraced the gospel as the very message they had been waiting for, and great numbers of them 'turned to the Lord' (Acts 11:21).

The Jerusalem apostles at this stage thought it their duty to supervise all forward movements of the faith, and when news of the outreach in Antioch came to them, they decided to send a representative to direct it and see that it did not get out of hand. It would have been a disaster had they sent some of the stricter judaizers of their company: as it was, they could not have made a wiser choice than they made. They sent Barnabas. On his arrival, Barnabas perhaps saw many excesses of religious enthusiasm that would have shocked some people. But he paid no attention to these. He concentrated on those features of the forward movement that called for encouragement: in particular, he rejoiced to see such abounding evidence of the grace of God at work. So he settled in Antioch and gave the new believers the leadership they needed.

But the work grew to a point where Barnabas felt that he could no longer superintend it unaided. Where, however, could he find a congenial colleague? He remembered his old friend Paul, who for the past ten years had been active as a missionary in and around his native Tarsus. He made a journey to Tarsus, found Paul, and persuaded him to go back with him to Antioch and help him in his ministry.

The two men spent an active and fruitful year together. It was in Antioch at this time, according

to Luke, that the followers of Jesus first came to be
called 'Christians' (Acts 11:26) – a designation which
could have been given to them only in a Gentile
environment.

It was Barnabas and Paul whom the young, and
predominantly Gentile, church of Antioch chose to
carry its gift of money to their fellow-believers in
Jerusalem when Judaea was hard hit by a famine. It
was perhaps in the course of this visit that the three
Jerusalem 'pillars' (James the Lord's brother, Peter
and John) agreed that Barnabas and Paul were as
truly called by God to the evangelization of Gentiles as
they themselves were to the evangelization of their
fellow-Jews (Gal. 2:1–10).[2]

Not long after their return to Antioch, the church
there was divinely directed to release Barnabas and
Paul for missionary service farther afield. The two
men, commended by the church for this extension of
their ministry, sailed for Cyprus and went through the
island from east to west, preaching the gospel in each
place where they stopped. Barnabas would have a
special interest in the evangelization of his native
island. From Paphos, the western capital of Cyprus,
they sailed north to the Anatolian coast. Soon after
they landed there, Barnabas's young cousin Mark,
whom they had brought from Jerusalem to Antioch
and then from Antioch on their present journey, left
them and went back to Jerusalem.[3] His reasons are not
stated: perhaps he felt that he had not expected to be
away so long, or perhaps he resented the way in which
Barnabas seemed to be falling into second place. So far
as Luke's narrative indicates, there might have been

[2] See *Men and Movements in the Primitive Church*, pp. 28–34, 90 f.
[3] See p. 75.

some substance to this: it was 'Barnabas and Saul' that set out from Antioch, but 'Paul and his company' that 'set sail from Paphos' (Acts 13:2, 13). However that might be, Barnabas had the special degree of grace celebrated by the rhymester:

> It takes more grace than I can tell
> To play the second fiddle well.

From the Anatolian coast Barnabas and Paul struck up country and preached the gospel in some of the leading cities of South Galatia – Pisidian Antioch, Iconium, Lystra and Derbe.[4] In each of these they planted churches and encouraged the new converts to stand firm in face of persecution and other forms of trial.

At Lystra they were attacked by a hostile populace: their horrified refusal to accept the divine honours which were being prepared for them no doubt gave deep offence. But an interesting light is thrown on the appearance and behaviour of the two missionaries by the statement that, when the people of Lystra took them to be deities visiting their city *incognito*, 'they called Barnabas Zeus, and Paul, because he was the chief speaker, they called Hermes' (Acts 14:12). There was apparently something majestic and dignified about the presence of Barnabas, that he should be identified with the father of gods and men; no one ever suggested that there was anything majestic about the appearance of the mercurial Paul.

When at last they returned to Antioch on the Orontes they had a great story to tell about 'all that God had done with them' (Acts 14:27).

---

[4] It is possible that Derbe (the modern Kerti Hüyük, near Karaman) lay across the south-eastern frontier of the province of Galatia, in the kingdom of Commagene, governed at this time by Rome's vassal Antiochus IV.

From Antioch Barnabas and Paul now paid a further visit to Jerusalem – this time to meet the apostles and elders who found it necessary to agree about the terms on which Gentile believers might be welcomed into church membership. Some Jewish Christians felt threatened by the rapid increase of Gentile converts. It was agreed that no terms could be required beyond those with which God had shown himself satisfied – faith in Jesus as Lord – but certain conditions were laid down which would make it easier for Jewish and Gentile Christians to enjoy table fellowship together.[5]

There had recently been a critical situation in the church of Antioch on this very issue. Representatives from Jerusalem persuaded Peter, who was on a visit to Antioch and enjoying table fellowship with Gentile Christians there, to withdraw from association with them. When 'even Barnabas' joined the other Jewish Christians who followed Peter's example of seating Jews and Gentiles at separate tables, Paul decided that a stern protest was called for (Gal. 2:11–14). We may be sure that Peter and Barnabas felt they had good reason for what they did – respecting the conscientious scruples of their weaker Judaean brethren, perhaps[6] – but we have not their side of the story. In retrospect we can conclude that Paul was right to protest, but the issue may not have been so clear at the time.

Luke says nothing of this dispute, but it is probable

---

[5] Acts 15:2–29; see p. 43.
[6] This is suggested by the fact that Peter's withdrawal from table fellowship with Gentiles took place after 'certain men came from James' (Gal. 2:12). What they said to him must be a matter of conjecture, but they may well have reported that news of what he was doing in Antioch was coming back to Jerusalem and causing scandal to the believers there as well as creating difficulties for the leaders of the mother-church in their missionary work among Jews.

that if Paul had not lost confidence in Barnabas then, the dispute which arose between them shortly afterwards, when Paul turned down Barnabas's proposal to take Mark along again on a return visit which they planned to pay to the churches of South Galatia, would not have been so bitter.[7] The two former colleagues had to part company. Barnabas took Mark and continued the evangelization of Cyprus which he and Paul had begun a few years before (Acts 15:36–39). The debt which Cyprus owes him is remembered to this day: the primate of the autocephalous Cypriot church is still reckoned to be his successor.[8] But more than that: Mark developed his spiritual potential under the guidance of his encouraging relative until the day came when even Paul acknowledged his usefulness in Christian service.[9]

Paul's last reference to Barnabas pays tribute to him as a likeminded minister of Christ (1 Cor. 9:6). In paying him this tribute, moreover, he implies that Barnabas, like Paul himself, preferred to be self-supporting rather than look for subsistence to his converts and other Christians. In this the two men appear to have been exceptions; most of the other Christian leaders availed themselves of the right that the Lord had laid down: 'that those who proclaim the gospel should get their living by the gospel' (1 Cor. 9:14). Indeed, those of them who were married expected - and most reasonably so - that their wives, when they accompanied them, should receive similar support.

[7] See p. 75.
[8] When the late Archbishop Makarios became first President of the Republic of Cyprus in 1960, it was remarked that he was simultaneously successor to both Barnabas and Sergius Paullus (Acts 13:7).
[9] See p. 76.

We have some idea of Paul's reasons for choosing not to exercise the right of being supported by his churches. Barnabas's reasons may have been the same; but we are not told. Obviously this common policy made it all the easier for the two men to work together: if one had accepted, or even requested, material support while the other refused it, invidious comparisons would have been drawn. It may even have been Barnabas's example that first influenced Paul in this respect: if Paul saw the policy in action in Barnabas's ministry, he would quickly appreciate its advantages.[10]

[10] See D.L. Dungan, *The Sayings of Jesus in the Churches of Paul* (Philadelphia: Fortress, 1971), pp. 27–40; G. Theissen, *The Social Setting of Early Christianity*, E.T. (T. & T. Clark, 1982), pp. 27–54.

3

Silas/Silvanus

It is clear that one and the same person appears in Acts under the name Silas and in Paul's letters under the name Silvanus. According to 1 Thessalonians, Silvanus was one of the group of three who brought the gospel to Thessalonica, the other two being Paul and Timothy. According to Acts 17:4, 10, Paul and Silas brought the gospel to Thessalonica (it is implied that Timothy was with them, although he is not explicitly named). The men whose names are given as joint-authors of 1 Thessalonians – 'Paul, Silvanus and Timothy' (1 Thess. 1:1) – say that at the time of visiting Thessalonica 'we had already suffered and been shamefully treated at Philippi' (1 Thess. 2:2); according to Acts 16:19–24 Paul and Silas were unjustly beaten with rods at Philippi and locked up overnight in the town jail. According to Paul in 2 Cor. 1:19, it was 'Silvanus and Timothy and I' that evangelized

Corinth; according to Acts 18:1–5, Paul arrived at Corinth alone from Athens but was rejoined soon afterwards by Silas and Timothy. Silvanus is a Latin name; Silas may have been a friendly abbreviation of it. It is quite characteristic of Paul in his letters to use the more formal name, while Luke prefers the familiar form current among a person's close acquaintances. It is possible that, just as Paul had a Jewish name, Saul, alongside his Latin name, so Silas was a Jewish name, corresponding to the Talmudic name *Shila*.

It would be tedious to refer to him constantly as Silas/Silvanus, so we shall content ourselves with calling him Silas.

Silas was a member of the church of Jerusalem, who was chosen by the leaders of that church, along with a colleague named Judas (of whom we know nothing further), to carry the apostolic letter of Acts 15:23–29 to Antioch. The letter was addressed 'to the brethren who are of the Gentiles in Antioch and Syria and Cilicia', assuring them that circumcision and submission to the Jewish law were not required of them before they could be recognized as members of the Christian community, but asking them to conform in certain respects to the Jewish way of life in order to make social fellowship between Jewish and Gentile believers easier. Since Antioch was the chief city of the united province of Syria-Cilicia, the delivery of the letter to the church there was the best way of ensuring that it would be read also by the daughter-churches throughout the province.

Not only did Judas and Silas deliver the letter to the Christians of Antioch; they stayed among them for some time, exercising their gift of prophecy and encouraging their Gentile brethren. Quite plainly they felt no misgivings about fraternizing with Gentiles, and were treated as welcome and honoured guests. Paul appears to have taken stock of Silas during those days and reached very positive conclusions about him. Judas and Silas in due course went back to Jerusalem, where they ranked as 'chief men among the brethren'. But when a little later, Paul and Barnabas parted company, Paul had no doubt whom he wished to co-opt as a colleague in place of Barnabas. Silas was persuaded to return to Antioch, and from there he and Paul set off on a journey which would take them not only to the Aegean shore of Asia Minor but across the sea to Europe.

Paul must have discerned qualities in Silas which made him a congenial companion and fellow-worker in the gospel enterprise. He certainly shared Paul's understanding of the law-free gospel, which extended the grace of God to Gentiles on an equal footing with Jews. Silas, no doubt, had been well pleased to carry the apostolic letter from Jerusalem to Antioch since he was in entire agreement with its terms. He belonged, evidently, to the more liberal wing of the Jerusalem church: 'if I may hazard a ... guess', wrote F.C. Burkitt, 'I should say that Silas had heard St. Stephen gladly'.[1]

Moreover, at this stage Paul could have found it useful to have a leader of the Jerusalem church as his colleague. It appears from the letter to the Galatians (which I should date several months earlier than the time of which we are speaking) that Paul was accused by some of his opponents of being out of step with the mother-church. But now, if any one should say, 'But

---

[1] F.C. Burkitt, *Christian Beginnings* (University of London Press, 1924), p. 13.

what do they think, or practise, at Jerusalem?' reply
could be made: 'Well, here is a leader of the Jerusalem
church; he can tell you authoritatively what is thought
or done there.' A modern reader, exaggerating the
tension between Paul and Jerusalem, might argue that
Silas was really sent with Paul to keep a watchful eye
on him, or that the church of Jerusalem wished
through his agency to maintain control over Paul's
Gentile mission. But such a reconstruction runs coun-
ter to Luke's understanding of the situation: according
to him 'Paul chose Silas' (Acts 15:40).

There may have been a further consideration in
Paul's mind when he chose Silas. It appears from the
account of their imprisonment in Philippi that Silas,
like Paul himself, was a Roman citizen. Paul protested
to the lictors, 'They have beaten us publicly, unconde-
mned, men who are Roman citizens'; and the magistrates 'were afraid when they heard that they were
Roman citizens' (Acts 16:37, 38). Roman citizenship
was not a prime requirement for association with Paul
(indeed, we do not know of any other fellow-
missionary of his who was a Roman citizen); but when
the more important qualities were present, Roman
citizenship had certain advantages. It meant, at least,
that Paul would not be in the embarrassing situation
where he could claim for himself privileges enjoyed by
a Roman citizen which his colleague could not claim.

Silas, having been co-opted by Paul as his colleague,
visited along with him the cities where Barnabas and
Paul had planted churches some two years before, and
at Lystra, one of these cities, they were joined by
Timothy. Silas experienced along with Paul the series
of checks to their western progress in which the
guidance of the Spirit was recognized, and turned

north-west with him (and Timothy) until they reached the port of Alexandria Troas. Here they were joined by the narrator of the story in Acts,[2] and (in response to Paul's night-vision in which he heard the call for help from 'a man of Macedonia') the party took ship for Neapolis (modern Kavalla), the port of Philippi. Silas then collaborated with Paul in gospel preaching and church planting in Philippi, Thessalonica, Beroea and Corinth.

If we ask why only Paul and Silas were arrested, beaten and imprisoned at Philippi, the answer may be that they were not only the leaders of the missionary party but were also full Jews, and may have been recognizable as such. (Luke was a Gentile,[3] and Timothy perhaps inherited the features of his Greek father.[4]) It is plain from the record that anti-Jewish feeling as well as concern for violated property rights played a part in the attack on Paul and Silas.

At Thessalonica, similarly, when the missionaries were charged before the city magistrates with being leaders of Jewish insurgency, it was Paul and Silas who were sent off by night to Beroea. At Beroea it was Paul who incurred most hostility; Silas was able to stay on there for a time with Timothy (who, it seems, was free to move without molestation and had travelled from Thessalonica to join his senior colleagues in Beroea).[5]

Silas's movements between Paul's departure from Beroea and his own arrival in Corinth from Macedonia to join Paul in this new area of apostolic activity

[2] This is indicated by the transition from 'he' and 'they' to 'we' in Acts 16:10. See p. 38.
[3] See p. 36.
[4] See p. 30.
[5] Acts 17:1–15.

can be pieced together only tentatively from occasional indications in Acts and 1 Thessalonians. During his time in Corinth he co-operated with Paul not only in gospel witness and church building but also, it appears, in the writing of 1 and 2 Thessalonians. There are signs in these letters, and especially in the former, that Silas's name appears in the prescript in no merely formal manner. There are places where Paul's voice in the first person singular is unmistakable, but the first person plural, 'we', is commoner, and it denotes especially Paul and Silas. (Timothy is also named in the prescript, but the statements in 1 Thess. 3:2, 6, 'we sent Timothy' and 'Timothy has come to us', imply that 'we' and 'us' are Paul and Silas.)[6]

It is possible that Silas had something to do with another of the New Testament letters. Towards the end of 1 Peter we read 'By Silvanus, a faithful brother as I regard him, I have written briefly to you' (1 Pet. 5:12). This Silvanus was probably the amanuensis employed in the writing down of 1 Peter, and responsible for its rather elegant Greek style; it may also have been he who carried the letter to the various provinces in Asia Minor where the addressees lived (1 Pet. 1:1). But there is nothing to show certainly whether or not he was identical with the Silas/Silvanus who at an earlier period participated in Paul's ministry.[7]

---

[6] See p. 32.
[7] E.G. Selwyn, *The First Epistle of St. Peter* (Macmillan, 1946), pp. 9–17, adduces certain data which 'raise some presumption that Silvanus played a large part in the authorship' of the Thessalonian correspondence and of 1 Peter.

4

Timothy of Lystra

Of all members of Paul's circle, there was none with whom he formed a closer mutual attachment than Timothy. In six of Paul's letters Timothy's name is associated with his own in the superscription; in four of these Timothy's name is the only one to be associated with Paul's in this way. This does not mean (except, just possibly, in Colossians)[1] that Timothy had any responsible share in the composition of the letter. He may have taken down the letter at Paul's dictation, but Paul does not give a man a place alongside himself in the superscription just because he was his amanuensis. Paul had other companions when he sent the letters in question, but Timothy's name is

[1] In the introductory thanksgivings to other letters (apart from 1 and 2 Thessalonians, which are of composite authorship) Paul says 'I thank God', even when Timothy or someone else is associated with himself in the prescript; in Col. 1:3, however, the wording is 'We thank God'. There are other indications that Timothy may have played a greater part in the writing of Colossians.

associated with his own because Timothy shared his ministry on a permanent footing.

Timothy's antecedents are indicated in Acts and the Pastoral Epistles. He was a native of Lystra (modern Zostera, near Hatunsaray), in the Lycaonian region of the province of Galatia. He was the son of a mixed marriage, his mother being a Jewess and his father a Greek. (The Jews of Anatolia were reputed to be laxer in such matters than Jews in many other parts of the Dispersion.) But his Jewish mother (Eunice by name) brought him up in her faith, with the added encouragement of her own mother Lois (2 Tim. 1:5); in particular, he was well versed from childhood in the OT scriptures, presumably in their Greek form (2 Tim. 3:15). He first appears in Luke's narrative when Paul (accompanied by Silas) pays his second visit to Lystra, returning to his Gentile mission-field after the Council of Jerusalem. By this time Timothy could be called a 'disciple..., the son of a Jewish woman who was a believer' (Acts 16:1); it appears, then, that mother and son had come to faith in Christ during Paul's previous visit to Lystra (in company with Barnabas), two or three years previously (Acts 14:6–20). That Timothy was a convert of Paul's is further implied by his description as Paul's 'true-born child in the faith' (1 Tim. 1:2).

Timothy's spiritual development had been rapid since his conversion: he was commended not only by responsible Christians in his own city but also by those in Iconium, about eighteen miles away. Paul quickly satisfied himself that their commendation was well founded, and decided that this youth had the qualities which would make him a very valuable assistant to him in his missionary and pastoral work. Timothy, for his part, was very willing to accompany Paul. He no doubt found something exceptionally captivating about Paul's personality: for his sake, and for the sake of the gospel to which Paul was dedicated, he was prepared to forget the ambitions which a young man of his gifts and opportunities could reasonably have cherished. His ready self-sacrifice and unfailing devotion were deeply appreciated by Paul.

As the son of a Jewish mother – one, moreover, who had himself been brought up in the Jewish faith – Timothy would have ranked as a genuine Jew, but for the fact that he had never been circumcised (no doubt his Gentile father would not hear of such a thing). To all practical intents and purposes he was a Jew in Gentile eyes, but in Jewish eyes he was worse than a Gentile – he was an apostate (because uncircumcised) Jew. Therefore, to regularize his status, Paul circumcised him. Had he not done so, as Martin Hengel says, he 'would have supported apostasy and would no longer have been allowed to appear in any synagogue.'[2] To Paul, circumcision in itself was a matter of complete indifference (Gal. 5:6; 6:15). What he objected to was circumcision imposed or accepted as a religious obligation or as necessary for salvation.

Timothy accompanied Paul (and Silas/Silvanus) west and north-west through Asia Minor to Troas, where they were joined by Luke. From there they set sail for Macedonia, landing at Neapolis (modern Kavalla) and going inland to Philippi. There Timothy saw some of the hazards attendant on apostolic activity – he had probably seen them already, although without personal involvement, when Paul was nearly

---

[2] M. Hengel, *Acts and the History of Earliest Christianity*, E.T. (SCM Press, 1979), p. 64.

stoned to death at Lystra on his first visit there. From
Philippi the missionary party went on to Thessalonica,
and after some weeks they had to leave that city in a
hurry. Paul was escorted for his own safety first to
Beroea and then on to Athens, and when Silvanus and
Timothy were able to rejoin him in Athens, Timothy
was sent back to Thessalonica to see how the young
church there was faring, and to give it the encouragement and reassurance it required in the midst of
persecution.[3] This was a responsible mission, and
Timothy must have been judged capable of discharging
it. He returned to join Paul in Corinth, bringing a good
report of the Thessalonian Christians' stability and
witness, which prompted the sending of 1 Thessalonians.

For the greater part of Paul's eighteen-months stay
in Corinth, and later of his three-years ministry in
Ephesus, Timothy appears to have been with him.
Paul's ministry in Ephesus was punctuated with dis-
quieting reports from his converts in Corinth, and in
his dealings with them he found Timothy's aid of great
value. He sent Timothy from Ephesus to Corinth
about the same time as the letter which we know as 1
Corinthians, to convey by word of mouth some of the
lessons emphasized in the letter (1 Cor. 4:17).
Timothy evidently set out before the letter was sent,
but might not arrive in Corinth until after it had been
received; presumably he was to visit other places as
well as Corinth. (This was probably the visit mentioned in Acts 19:22; if so, Timothy was to include
Macedonia in his itinerary.) Paul thought it necessary

---

[3] It was Paul who took the initiative in sending him (1 Thess. 3:5), but Silvanus
concurred: they speak of Timothy as 'our brother and God's servant in the gospel
of Christ' (1 Thess. 3:2). See p. 28.

to urge the Corinthians not to despise Timothy but put him at his ease among them (1 Cor. 16:10, 11); it may be gathered that Timothy's personality was not forceful enough to cope with the self-confidence of some members of the church of Corinth.

Timothy was with Paul in Corinth a year or two later when the Epistle to the Romans was despatched (Rom. 16:21), and he was one of the large party that accompanied Paul on his last voyage to Judaea (Acts 20:4). After Paul's arrest in Jerusalem we lose sight of Timothy, but he reappears with Paul in Rome, if the captivity epistles were composed there (Phil. 1:1; Col. 1:1; Philem. 1). When Paul had reason to believe that a judicial decision would soon be taken about him in the imperial court, he wrote to his Philippian friends telling them that, as soon as he knew the outcome, he would send Timothy to give them the news and to bring him back news of them. It is at this point that he gives Timothy a quite remarkable encomium: 'I have no one like him, who will be genuinely anxious for your welfare. They all look after their own interests, not those of Jesus Christ. But Timothy's worth you know, how as a son with a father he has served with me in the gospel' (Phil. 2:20–22).

If Timothy was actually Paul's amanuensis for this letter, he must have blushed as he took down these words. These words, it may be thought, do not set Paul's other companions in a very good light. But consider what he was asking Timothy to undertake – a forty-days journey on foot from Rome to Philippi (with the short sea-crossing of the Straits of Otranto) and another forty-days journey back. There were not many of his friends whom he could expect to do that for him; but he knew that Timothy would do it willingly. A few verses above he has entreated the Philippian Christians to emulate the self-denying mind 'which was also in Christ Jesus' (Phil. 2:5); here in Timothy they had a living example of one who manifested that mind (and another example is provided by Epaphroditus, who is commended in the next paragraph).[4]

All the affection which a father could feel for a likeminded son Paul felt for Timothy, and in return he received from Timothy all the service and devotion which a son could give to a father.

On one occasion Paul gave Timothy a responsible commission to be fulfilled in the Ephesian church (1 Tim. 1:3); later he sent him a message from his condemned cell, begging him to come to him with all haste and to collect on the way the cloak, books and parchments which he had left at Troas some time before (2 Tim. 4:6–12). We do not know if Timothy reached Rome in time to see the apostle alive.

Nor do we know if it was before this, or at a rather later date, that Timothy himself was imprisoned for the gospel's sake. 'Our brother Timothy', we read in the personal notes with which the Epistle to the Hebrews is concluded, 'has been released, with whom I shall see you if he comes soon' (Heb. 13:23).[5] The place and circumstances of this imprisonment must remain obscure; Timothy, as we take our leave of him, continues to be involved in the activities and hazards of the gospel ministry.

[4] See p. 84.
[5] In 'Our Brother Timothy', *Evangelical Quarterly* 40 (1968), pp. 220–223, J.D. Legg puts forward the suggestion that Timothy was the writer to the Hebrews; that he sent the letter because, being in custody, he was unable to pay a personal visit to the recipients; and that Heb. 13:22–25 should be recognized as the 'few words' appended by someone else (Paul himself, he thinks), inviting the readers' acceptance of the 'word of exhortation' (the letter as a whole) and including the last-minute news that Timothy (the author) had just been released from custody.

5

Luke, the Beloved Physician

Luke plays no prominent part by name in the New Testament. He is mentioned three times in Paul's later letters as one of his companions.[1]

The most informative of these three mentions comes in Col. 4:14, 'Luke the beloved physician and Demas greet you.' From this we gather what Luke's profession was, but we gather more than that. Writing from his place of imprisonment (in Rome, probably) to the Christians of Colossae, a city in Phrygia, Paul sends greetings from six men who are with him when the letter is ready to be despatched. He names them in two groups of three. Of the first three – Aristarchus, Mark and Jesus surnamed Justus – he says, 'These are the only men of the circumcision among my fellow-

---

[1] His name (Greek *Loukas*) is probably an abbreviation of the Latin Lucius, but he cannot be identified with either of the two bearers of that name mentioned elsewhere in the New Testament (Acts 13:1; Rom. 16:21).

workers for the kingdom of God' (Col. 4:11). We conclude that these were his only Jewish-Christian associates who were in his company at the time. We conclude, accordingly, that the next three companions mentioned – Epaphras, Luke and Demas – were Gentile Christians. In the letter to Philemon, sent at the same time and to the same place as Colossians, greetings are sent from five of those six 'fellow-workers', and Luke is one of them. At a later time, in a passage evidently written on the eve of his execution, Paul says, 'Luke alone is with me' (2 Tim. 4:11). If Luke alone was with him, it is not difficult to decide that Luke must have served as his amanuensis while those words were dictated.[2]

But, according to a strong tradition going back to the second century, Luke played a much more important part in the New Testament than those brief references would indicate: he was responsible for two of the most important documents in the New Testament – the Third Gospel and the Acts of the Apostles – which together make up a valuable history of Christian origins, covering a period of more than sixty years, from the conception and birth of John the Baptist to Paul's Roman imprisonment (his *first* Roman imprisonment, if he endured more than one).

What is the strength of this tradition? Luke plays such an insignificant part by name in the New Testament that there is no reason why he should have been picked on arbitrarily as the author of the two longest literary works in the whole collection. If their author was quite unknown, and it was thought fit to assign an appropriate name to him, it might have been expected

---

[2] It has even been held that he was the author of the three Pastoral Epistles; cf.

that an apostle or some prominent figure in primitive Christian history would have been selected. The tradition that Luke was their author, which can be traced in writing in the second century, probably went back orally to the first century: people *remembered* that he composed the two works.

It was argued at one time that the medical element in the vocabulary of Luke and Acts shows that their author was a physician.[3] This argument has been exaggerated; the evidence is indeed consistent with his having been a physician, but to conclude that he *must* have been a physician is to perpetrate the fallacy of some students of Shakespeare who have argued, from the legal element in the vocabulary of the plays, that they must have been written by a lawyer (meaning Francis Bacon).[4]

Is there anything in the contents of Luke or Acts – more particularly, of Acts – to indicate that the author was or was not one of Paul's companions (as he must have been, if he was Luke)? One of my British colleagues, for whose judgment in matters of New Testament scholarship I have very high respect, has said that 'on any showing' it is unlikely that the author of the complete work (Luke and Acts) 'knew Paul personally'.[5] But on this matter my own judgment, for what it is worth, is quite contrary to his.

Although both the Third Gospel and Acts are anonymous, the author speaks of himself as 'I' in the opening sentence of both works. 'I for my part have

---

S.G. Wilson, *Luke and the Pastoral Epistles* (SPCK, 1979).

[3] Cf. W.K. Hobart, *The Medical Language of St. Luke* (Dublin University Press, 1882).

[4] Cf. H.J. Cadbury, *Style and Literary Method of Luke* (Cambridge, Mass.: Harvard Theological Studies 6, 1920), pp. 39–72.

[5] C.K. Barrett, 'Acts and the Pauline Corpus', *Expository Times* 88 (1976–77), p. 4.

decided to write', he tells Theophilus in Luke 1:3; 'I wrote my former account', he tells him in Acts 1:1 as he refers back to the Third Gospel. These are not the only places where he uses the first personal pronoun, but elsewhere he uses the plural 'we'. It is most natural to suppose that the plural 'we' includes the singular 'I'. If so, then the author of the twofold work is the narrator of the three 'we' passages of Acts (as they are called) – that is to say, the passages, beginning in Acts 16:10; 20:5 and 27:1, where the third-personal record ('they', 'them') gives way to a first-personal record ('we', 'us').[6]

If the author of the complete work was not a companion of Paul, then it would have to be concluded that he has incorporated extracts from someone else's diary in his work, or even (as some suggest) that the diary style is a literary device calculated to lend vividness and verisimilitude to the narrative.[7] But here the most natural explanation of the 'we' passages is most likely to be the true one.

If that is so – if the change from 'they' to 'we' indicates that at these points Luke himself joined the company – then we can construct something of his history from the record of Acts. He joined Paul, Silas and Timothy at Troas in A.D. 50 and travelled with them to Philippi (Acts 16:10–18). When the three others left Philippi, he appears to have been left behind; it is at Philippi that he rejoined Paul and a number of other companions (actually, representatives of Gentile churches who were taking those churches'

---

[6] Cf. H.J. Cadbury, '"We" and "I" Passages in Luke–Acts', *New Testament Studies* 3 (1955–57), pp. 128–132, for a particularly convincing argument.

[7] Cf. E. Haenchen, *The Acts of the Apostles*, E.T. (Oxford: Blackwell, 1971), pp. 85–87, 490 f.

contributions to Jerusalem to be handed over to the leaders of the mother-church),[8] and he sailed with them to Caesarea and completed the journey to Jerusalem (Acts 20:5–21: 18). Two years later he joined Paul at Caesarea and accompanied him on his adventurous voyage, experiencing the shipwreck at Malta, wintering on that island, going on then by sea to Puteoli and by land to Rome (Acts 27:1–28: 16).

Perhaps he remained in Philippi during the interval of seven years between the first and second 'we' passages; it is even conceivable that he is the 'true yokefellow' whom Paul asks in Phil 4:3 to lend a helping hand to Euodia and Syntyche.[9] During Paul's two years in custody at Caesarea (between the second and third 'we' passages), Luke was probably not far away; a reasonable supposition is that he spent part of the time collecting information which in due course he included in his Gospel and the earlier part of Acts.

It is interesting to note that the three 'we' passages are largely devoted to day-to-day recordings of journeys by sea. Their author looked at the sea through the eyes of a Greek, for whom it was a natural (if at times over-boisterous) element.

Possibly Luke is referred to in other places where his name is not given. A tradition going back to the first half of the third century identifies him with the unnamed 'brother' who accompanied Titus on his mission to Corinth in connexion with the Jerusalem relief fund (2 Cor. 8:18f.; 12:18);[10] this tradition

---

[8] See p. 98.

[9] This identification is bound up with the dating of Philippians, or at least of this section of it; the question is briefly discussed in my 'Good News Commentary' on *Philippians* (San Francisco: Harper & Row, 1983), pp. 113–115. On Euodia, Syntyche and the 'yokefellow' see further pp. 85, 94f. below.

[10] On the suggestion that Luke and Titus were brothers see p. 64.

persists in the Collect for St. Luke's Day with its mention of 'Luke the physician, whose praise is in the gospel'. But this is quite uncertain.

A better attested tradition makes Luke a native of Antioch in Syria. This tradition, indeed, has found a place in the 'western' text of Acts 11:28 where, before the statement that Agabus rose to prophesy, comes an inserted clause: 'when we were gathered together'. This cannot be taken as the original reading, but it bears witness to the antiquity of the tradition. A more incidental piece of evidence has been detected in Acts 6:5, where the seven men elected as almoners in the Jerusalem church are named, and the only one whose place of origin is mentioned, the proselyte Nicolaus, is said to have come from Antioch. This has been thought to reflect a special interest in Antioch on the part of the narrator.[11]

If Luke was a Gentile, then he was probably the only Gentile among the writers of the New Testament (indeed, of the whole Bible). It would not be surprising to learn that, before he became a Christian, he was a 'God-fearer'[12] – that is, a Gentile loosely attached to the Jewish synagogue, who would already have some familiarity with the Old Testament writings (in Greek) and with the levitical calendar.

By his own account, he wrote his history in order to provide one Theophilus with an orderly and reliable

[11] J. Smith, *The Voyage and Shipwreck of St. Paul* (Longmans, ⁴1880), p. 4, notes as a parallel that, out of eight accounts of Napoleon's Russian campaign of 1812 – three by Frenchmen, three by Englishmen and two by Scots – only the two Scots writers mention that the Russian general Barclay de Tolly was of Scots extraction.
[12] This is not a technical term, but Luke commonly describes Gentile members of a synagogue congregation thus. Cf. A.T. Kraabel, 'The Disappearance of the God-fearers', *Numen* 28 (1981), pp. 113–126; M. Wilcox, 'God-fearers in Acts', *Journal for the Study of the New Testament* 13 (1981), pp. 102–122.

record of the rise and progress of the Christian faith. Theophilus may well have been a representative of the intelligent reading public of Rome, who would be interested to have a trustworthy account of a sect that was 'everywhere spoken against'. While the perspective of the completed work appears to be that of a rather later date, it has been held by some students that the first draft was compiled in order to supply an authoritative 'document in the case' for the officials who were responsible for preparing the agenda for the hearing of Paul's appeal in the imperial court.[13] (There is, of course, much in the completed work that would be irrelevant for such a purpose.)

'Luke', says a prologue to the Third Gospel whose contents may go back to the second century, 'was an Antiochian of Syria, a physician by profession. He was a disciple of the apostles and later accompanied Paul until his martyrdom. He served the Lord without distraction, having neither wife nor children, and at the age of eighty-four he fell asleep in Boeotia, full of the Holy Spirit.'[14]

Luke devotes his literary skill and historical research to a worthy cause and has served posterity well. While the first part of his record of Christian origins is largely paralleled in the other Gospels, he has preserved valuable material not found in them. In the early part of his Gospel we have the annunciation of the births of John the Baptist and Jesus, the canticles

---

[13] G.S. Duncan, *St. Paul's Ephesian Ministry* (Hodder & Stoughton, 1929), p. 97, asks: 'What more probable motive can Luke have had than to prepare a statement of the rise and development of the Christian religion, designed to supply information which it was hoped might reach those who would decide the apostle's fate at Rome?'

[14] The so-called Anti-Marcionite Prologue to Luke, translated in full in F.F. Bruce, *The Spreading Flame* (Paternoster, [2]1982), pp. 230 f.

of Mary, Zechariah and Simeon, the overcrowded inn at Bethlehem, the angelic appearance to the shepherds, the shepherds' visit to the infant Saviour, his presentation in the temple, and his presence in the temple twelve years later at Passovertide. In the passion and resurrection narrative at the end of the Gospel we have the Lord's hearing before Herod Antipas, his prayer for the forgiveness of his executioners, his words of assurance to the penitent robber, his appearance alive from the dead to the two disciples on the Emmaus road. In the body of the work we have the parables of the good Samaritan, the prodigal son, the rich man and Lazarus, the Pharisee and the tax-collector. For all the debt we owe to the other evangelists, we should have been much the poorer had Luke not given us his account.

As for the second part of his record, we have only to compare our knowledge of the first thirty years of the church's life with our ignorance of the next thirty years – or indeed of the next hundred and thirty years – to realize something of our indebtedness to him. There is much we should like to know even of the first thirty years that he does not tell us, but we may well be grateful for what he does tell us, tracing the course of events accurately from the first. We should like to know how the gospel advanced along other roads than that which led from Jerusalem to Rome; but at least, thanks to Luke, we do know something of its progress along that most important of roads.

Along that road the most active gospel preacher was Paul, apostle to the Gentiles. It is no exaggeration to say that Paul is the hero of Acts. We know Paul rather well from his own writings, but in Acts we can view him through the eyes of another, who wrote without any dependence on Paul's letters. (It would be rash to say that Luke did not know any of Paul's letters, but he shows no sign of knowing them, and they cannot be included among the sources of which he availed himself.)

Admirers of Paul tend to depreciate other Christian leaders of the same generation, such as Peter and James the Just. Luke is an admirer of Paul, but he does no injustice to Peter and James. It is Peter who first opens a door of salvation to Gentiles, by visiting the house of Cornelius (reluctantly at first) to tell the story of Jesus there.[15] Peter comes down unambiguously on the side of gospel liberty in Luke's account of the Council of Jerusalem.[16] On the same occasion James shows his statesmanlike quality as he sums up the sense of the meeting.[17] Luke is a truly catholic writer; he knows that there were various strands in primitive Christianity, and he weaves them together in the interests of Christian unity – a cause obviously dear to his heart.

[15] Acts 10:9–11: 17.
[16] Acts 15:7-11.
[17] Acts 15:13–21; cf. pp. 20, 24.

6

Priscilla and Aquila

There are some married couples of whom their friends call to mind the wife first, and immediately thereafter they remember that there is a husband too. This need not always be indicated by mentioning her name before his: it is customary, for example, to speak of Sidney and Beatrice Webb, but Beatrice, by all accounts, was the more impressive personality of the two.

Priscilla and Aquila are mentioned six times in the New Testament – three times in the Pauline letters and three times in Acts. Each writer, Paul and Luke, puts Priscilla before her husband in two out of the three places where he names them. On the two occasions when Paul puts Priscilla first (except that he prefers to call her Prisca) he sends his greetings to them (Rom. 16:3; 2 Tim. 4:19); on the other occasion, writing to the Corinthian Christians from Ephesus, he

said, 'Aquila and Prisca send their warm greetings
in the Lord' (1 Cor. 16:19). He may well have been in
their home at the time, and as he wrote, or rather
dictated, it is quite credible that Priscilla insisted that
her husband's name be put first.

As for Luke, he puts Aquila's name first when he
tells how Paul, soon after he arrived in Corinth 'found
a Jew named Aquila, lately come from Italy with his
wife Priscilla' (Acts 18:2). It was Aquila's name that
would have been written over the entrance to the
tent-making workshop which he had newly set up in
that city.[1]

Paul speaks of Prisca, not Priscilla. This is in line
with his habit of referring to people by their formal
names (in his letters, at any rate); Luke refers to them
by their more familiar names. Thus Paul says Silvanus
where Luke says Silas; Paul says Sosipater where Luke
says Sopater.[2] But when he speaks of Prisca, he
reminds us of an ancient and illustrious Roman family,
the *gens Prisca*. It is conceivable that the wife of Aquila
belonged in some way to that family; if so, she would
have come from a much higher social level than her
husband. Such marriages are attested in early Christianity – even marriages between freewomen and slaves
(although that was not the situation here). Paul's
insistence that social distinctions lost their relevance
within the Christian fellowship was not peculiar to
him: it inhered in the logic of Christian faith and life.
But in the secular society of the time, when one finds a
wife being named before her husband, the reason
usually is that her social status was higher than his.

[1] The word which literally means 'tent-maker' (*skēnopoios*) may have the wider
sense of 'leather-worker'.
[2] See pp. 23f., 98.

The Cemetery of Priscilla on the Via Salaria in Rome is called after a noble Roman lady at the end of the first or beginning of the second century A.D.; but there is no evidence to connect her with the Priscilla of the New Testament. Many of the burials in this cemetery are of Christian members of a senatorial family bearing the name Acilius Glabrio,[3] which owned property in the vicinity. Any resemblance between the name Acilius and that of our Priscilla's husband is fortuitous.

Priscilla and Aquila are nowhere claimed by Paul as converts of his. They were probably Christians by the time he made their acquaintance; that is to say, they were probably Christians before they left Rome. In 1900 the German church historian, Adolf Harnack, argued that they were foundation members of the Roman church.[4] I believe he was right. They left Rome when the Emperor Claudius issued an edict expelling all Jews from the city – an edict which, it appears, should be dated in A.D. 49. One Roman writer who mentions the edict says it was issued because the Jews of Rome were engaging in constant riots 'at the instigation of Christ'[5] – writing over sixty years after the event, he gives a garbled and unintelligent account of the fact that the introduction of Christianity led to riots in the synagogues of Rome, as it did in many other cities of the Roman Empire. Priscilla may not have come personally within the

---

[3] An earlier Acilius Glabrio, consul in A.D. 91, was put to death by the Emperor Domitian four years later on a charge of Judaism and atheism – which might imply Christianity: one cannot be sure (Suetonius, *Lives of the Twelve Caesars: Domitian* 10.2; Dio Cassius, *History* 67.14).

[4] A. Harnack, 'Probabilia über die Adresse und den Verfasser des Hebräerbriefs', *Zeitschrift für die Neutestamentliche Wissenschaft* 1 (1900), pp. 16–41. In the same article Harnack suggested that Priscilla was the author of the letter to the Hebrews.

[5] Suetonius, *Lives of the Twelve Caesars: Claudius* 25.4.

scope of the expulsion edict – she may not have been Jewish by birth – but she went into exile with her husband. He was an immigrant Jew from Pontus, on the Black Sea coast of Asia Minor. Paul joined them in Corinth because their trade was the same as his, and they could provide him with work which would enable him, as he preferred, to earn his own living while he preached the gospel free of charge. But he and they had more important things in common than this. A firm and lasting friendship speedily grew up between them, and Paul was not slow in acknowledging his indebtedness to them.

When he had completed eighteen months in Corinth (say, from the autumn of A.D. 50 to the spring of 52), he left that city and crossed the Aegean to Asia. Priscilla and Aquila went with him and settled in Ephesus. They have been envisaged as the kind of business people who had branches in several cities. They may have left a manager in charge of their Roman branch (the original headquarters) when they could no longer stay in Rome, and another manager in charge of their Corinthian branch when they moved to Ephesus and set up yet another branch there. Paul did not stay in Ephesus on that occasion; after a few days he set out by sea for a visit to Judaea and Syria, promising to return to Ephesus later.

During his absence, Priscilla and Aquila made the acquaintance of a very interesting Jewish traveller named Apollos, from Alexandria in Egypt. Apollos was a sufficiently important member of the Pauline circle to merit separate treatment, which he shall have in our next chapter. For the moment, it must suffice to say that Priscilla and Aquila were impressed by the ready eloquence with which he expounded the Old

Testament scriptures in the synagogue, arguing that
their prophecies regarding the Messiah had found
their fulfilment in Jesus. Such exposition was a sheer
delight to the couple, but they spotted certain deficiencies in his understanding of 'the Way' (as the young
Christian movement was sometimes called by those
who belonged to it), so they invited him to their home
and made good those deficiencies. No doubt they
themselves had learned much from their association
with Paul.[6]

In the late summer of A.D. 52 Paul returned to
Ephesus from Syria by land, to embark on one of the
most fruitful phases of his apostolic ministry. During
his time in Ephesus, which lasted for the best part of
three years, he had quite a number of fellow-workers,
and none whose co-operation he valued more highly
than Priscilla and Aquila's. When, writing to the
Christians in Corinth (their old friends as well as his),
he sent greetings from Priscilla and Aquila, he sent
greetings also from 'the church in their house' (1 Cor.
16:19). It appears, then, that they made their house in
Ephesus available as a meeting-place for one group in
the rapidly growing church of that city.

It was probably in Ephesus, too, that they were
involved along with Paul in a situation which was
fraught with danger both for him and for them. When,
a year or two after the end of his time in Ephesus, he
sent greetings to them in his letter to the Christians in
Rome, he mentions that for his sake they once risked
their necks (Rom. 16:4). There is plenty of evidence
that Paul, during his years in Ephesus, was exposed to

---

[6] In Acts 18:26, where this is related, the editor of the 'western' text, followed by
others, changed the order from 'Priscilla and Aquila' to 'Aquila and Priscilla'; he
may have felt that it was unfitting that a woman should take the lead in a teaching
minstry. Today some would put that editor down as a male chauvinist.

hazards of which the merest allusions have come down
to us. The only one which is described in detail is the
riot in the Ephesian theatre, which in fact seems to
have been more perilous for some of Paul's associates
than for himself (Acts 19:23–40). In one of those
dangerous situations, then, Priscilla and Aquila risked
their lives for the apostle, and he could not forget their
devotion. We should dearly love to know the details,
but they are hidden from us. The Yiddish novelist
Sholem Asch, in his sympathetic and gripping romance *The Apostle*, describes how Paul, ignoring the
Asiarchs' friendly warning, was determined to face the
hostile crowd in the theatre when Priscilla picked him
up, tucked him under her arm, and carried him off to
safety – but this is a flight of imagination which the
earthbound historian can admire but not imitate! The
occasion to which Paul refers could perhaps have had
something to do with the deadly peril which he once
underwent 'in Asia', according to 2 Cor. 1:8–10 – but
we must be content with saying that we do not know. I
once heard a preacher make note of the fact that
Priscilla and Aquila are said to have 'risked their *neck*',
in the singular – a matter of Greek idiom – and try to
explain that, in some metaphysical sense, husband
and wife share but one neck; but I have forgotten the
precise terms of his explanation, so I cannot pass it on
to others.

By the time Paul wrote to the Romans, Priscilla and
Aquila had returned to Rome. It is plain that by this
time (early in A.D. 57) Claudius's edict of expulsion
had been allowed to lapse; since 54 a new emperor had
been on the throne. In Rome, as in Ephesus, Priscilla
and Aquila had a 'church in their house', to which also
Paul's greetings are sent. It is evident that, although

he had never been in Rome, Paul was not ignorant of conditions among the Christians there; no doubt from time to time messages had reached him from Priscilla and Aquila which kept him informed of the situation which he might expect to find when his planned visit to the capital took place. When, after unexpected delays, he did at last reach Rome, there is no indication whether they were still resident there or not. But they played a notable part in Paul's missionary enterprise: 'to them', his tribute ran, 'not only I give thanks, but also all the churches of the Gentiles' (Rom. 16:4).

7

Apollos of Alexandria

It is surprising how ill-informed we are about the
beginnings of Christianity in Egyptian Alexandria,
when one considers the important part that the church
of that city was destined to play in Christian history
from the second century to the seventh. All that the
New Testament has to say about Alexandrian Christianity is concerned with one man, and even he figures
but briefly in the record. That one man is Apollos, who
is mentioned several times by Paul in 1 Corinthians
and is the subject of a paragraph in Acts.[1] There is a
passing reference to him in the personal notes at the
end of the letter to Titus, which makes no substantial
additon to our knowledge of him.

A proper regard for historical method in the compa-
rative study of documents would lead us to examine
Paul's account of the man first, and then that given by

[1] The 'western' text of Acts gives Apollonius as the fuller form of his name.

Luke (since Paul's account is earlier, and based on
personal acquaintance, whereas we have no means of
knowing if Luke and Apollos ever met). But when we
have studied the documents in chronological order, we
find that Luke provides so apt a narrative setting for
Paul's references that we can now summarize his
narrative by way of background to what Paul has to
say.

Apollos, then, was a member of the very large
Jewish community of Alexandria. He was 'an eloquent
man, well versed in the scriptures' (Acts 18:24), and if
the NIV rendering 'a learned man' be preferred to the
RSV 'an eloquent man', it does not matter much: he
was probably both.[2] He appears to have been an
itinerant Jew of a type not uncommon in the first
Christian century – a commercial traveller who engaged in religious teaching as well as in trade.
Josephus tells of two Jews of this type who, some ten
years earlier than the date at which Apollos appears in
our records, were responsible for the conversion to
Judaism and subsequent instruction in that faith of the
royal family of Adiabene, east of the Tigris.[3] But this
itinerant Jew was not only well versed in the Old
Testament writings: he had become attached to 'the
Way' and had an accurate knowledge of the story of
Jesus. So, when he visited synagogues as he went from
city to city and was invited to expound the scriptures,
he argued that Jesus was the Messiah to whom the
prophets pointed fowards. He did so in the synagogue
of Ephesus in the summer of AD 52, at the time when
Priscilla and Aquila had recently moved to that city

[2] The adjective *logios* meant 'learned' in classical Greek, but came to mean
'eloquent' in Hellenistic and modern Greek.
[3] Josephus, *Antiquities* 20.34–48.

from Corinth. (Paul, who had travelled from Corinth to Ephesus with them, had gone on to pay a visit to Syria and Judaea.)

Priscilla and Aquila heard this man speak in the synagogue, and immediately recognized that he shared their faith. But, as they listened to his public exposition, or talked with him at other times, they became aware of some gaps in his knowledge of the gospel: 'he knew only the baptism of John' (Acts 18:25). So they invited him to their home for further conversation, and were able to fill in the gaps in his knowledge.

His ignorance of baptism in Jesus' name, first administered on the day of Pentecost (coupled perhaps with ignorance of other aspects of the Pentecostal experience), raises questions about the source of his knowledge of 'the Way'. According to the 'western' text of Acts, he had come to know it in his native city. This is not improbable, but who first brought the gospel to Alexandria? One might suppose that it was brought to Alexandria, as it was brought to Antioch, by refugees from the persecution which broke out in Judaea after Stephen's martyrdom; but it may be thought unlikely that missionaries from Jerusalem should be ignorant of Christian baptism. The Christian Hellenists, however, were a varied band, and some could have been less well-versed in the foundations of the faith than others.

In the next paragraph of Acts to that in which Apollos is introduced we meet some 'disciples' at Ephesus who were not only unaware of Christian baptism but had not even heard about the coming of the Holy Spirit (Acts 19:1–7). But we cannot conclude that Apollos shared their ignorance of the Holy Spirit.

What is meant by the statement in Acts 18:25 that he was 'fervent in spirit'? The same phrase appears in Rom. 12:11, where RSV renders it 'aglow with the Spirit'. This might be a true description of Apollos; we cannot be certain whether the phrase in Acts 18:25 means this or denotes Apollos's natural enthusiasm.

In due course Apollos's business took him across the Aegean Sea to Corinth, where as a matter of course he would visit the synagogue and be as active there as he had been in the synagogue of Ephesus. But Priscilla and Aquila knew that he could be very helpful also to the church in Corinth, so (along with some other Christians, it appears, who were at that time in Ephesus), they sent a letter to their Christian friends in Corinth urging them to give Apollos a welcome. This they did, and learned to appreciate him highly. At the same time he made an impact in the Jewish community of Corinth. It was a delicate matter to mention the name of Jesus in the Corinthian synagogue, from which Paul had been virtually ejected not long before for his persistence in 'inserting the name of the Lord Jesus' into the scripture readings (as the 'western' text of Acts 18:4 affirms). But perhaps Apollos had a way with him, for although 'he powerfully confuted the Jews in public, showing by the scriptures that the Messiah was Jesus' (Acts 18:28), no such trouble is said to have broken over his head as over Paul's.

Luke's account, then, is just the background we need to understand Paul's references to Apollos in 1 Corinthians. Such was the appreciation with which Apollos's teaching was received in the church of Corinth that some of its members felt he was the man for them. If other members of the church had their favourite teachers, these people had no doubt about theirs: they were of Apollos's school. Perhaps they felt that Apollos was eloquent, as Paul (by his own account) was not; perhaps, too, Apollos indulged in the imaginative allegorization which marked one illustrious and influential leader in Alexandrian Judaism (the philosopher Philo) to a point where some of his hearers felt that Paul's ministry was pedestrian and superficial by comparison.

Paul for his part appreciated the help which Apollos gave to the Corinthian Christians after his own departure from their city. He knew that there was nothing faulty about the foundation he himself had laid. But he warned others to be careful about the quality of the materials they used for building on the one true foundation. Of the quality of Apollos's materials, however, he had no complaint to make. The architectural metaphor was not the only one he employed to describe his work and that of his successors; he also spoke of the church in Corinth as God's field. He first came and sowed the good seed in the field, and then Apollos came and watered it. God acknowledged the workmanship of both men by making the seed sprout and produce a harvest. Paul did, however, deplore the way in which some of his converts impoverished themselves by looking to one only of the servants of Christ as their approved teacher, when Paul and Apollos and Peter and others were all given to them to profit by. It was just as bad, from his point of view, when others out of a well-meant sense of loyalty to the apostle who first brought the gospel to them thought of themselves as Paul's disciples. 'What is Apollos, and what is Paul? Servants (of Christ), through whom you came to faith' (1 Cor. 3:5).

It is clear that there was complete confidence between Paul and Apollos. This is evident from the way in which Paul cites Apollos and himself by way of pointing an example. When a speaker or writer refers to someone else by name along with himself to illustrate some aspect of personal relations, he will (if he is wise) choose someone who will not take offence by being singled out in this way. Paul may apply a certain lesson to Apollos and himself in order to bring home to his Corinthian friends something which they need to learn; he does not use Peter's name with the same freedom. There was, moreover, no question of apostolic rivalry betwen Paul and Apollos in the minds of their self-styled followers, for no one could consider Apollos an apostle in any sense. But Peter was undoubtedly an apostle, and those who enrolled themselves under his leadership might be tempted to think that, after all, his apostolic credentials were much more 'substantial' than Paul's. Had he not been a leading disciple of Jesus throughout his ministry?

From the way in which Paul speaks of Apollos, he appears to have known him personally: where did they meet? In Ephesus, probably, if Apollos paid a second visit there during Paul's Ephesian ministry. That Apollos did visit Ephesus while Paul was there is the natural inference from 1 Cor. 16:12, another passage which bears witness to Paul's confidence in him. Writing to the Corinthians from Ephesus, Paul says, 'With regard to our brother Apollos, I urged him strongly to come to you with the brethren' (i.e. with Stephanas, Fortunatus and Achaicus, who had visited Paul from Corinth and were now about to set out for home again). 'However', Paul goes on, 'it was not at all his will to come now; he will come when he has a favourable opportunity.' It is not clear whether 'his will' means 'Apollos's will' or 'God's will'; in any case, Paul would not have urged Apollos to visit Corinth if he suspected that he would make trouble there or lead the believers astray.

Of the reference to Apollos in Tit. 3:13 not much can be said, except that he appears to have paid a visit to Crete (along with an otherwise unknown lawyer named Zenas), and Titus is requested to see that he is supplied with everything he needs when he sets out on his further journey from there.

Much more might be said about Apollos, if there is any truth in the idea first ventilated by Luther in 1537 and supported by many students since then – that he was the author of the letter to the Hebrews.[4] On this all that need be said here is that the author was certainly a person of sacred learning, well-versed in the OT scriptures, and probably of Alexandrian origin. But it is only our ignorance that makes us unaware of others in the apostolic age, in addition to Apollos, who could be described in those terms.

We are grateful nevertheless for the brief glimpse that is given us of this Jew from Alexandria, this man of culture, with a mastery of the scriptures and an accurate knowledge of the story of Jesus, who for a short time traverses the Pauline circle, endearing himself to its members and to the apostle himself, makes a powerful impression on Jews and Christians in Ephesus and Corinth, and then disappears from our sight.[5]

---

[4] In a sermon on 1 Cor. 3:4–6; he repeated the idea in his *Commentary on Genesis* (1545).

[5] See also *Men and Movements in the Primitive Church*, pp. 65–80.

8

Titus of Antioch

Titus is mentioned only occasionally in the letters of Paul, but it is plain that he was a member of the circle who enjoyed Paul's confidence and appreciation in an exceptional degree.

I have called him 'Titus of Antioch', but that is an inference from the first occasion on which he is mentioned. In Gal. 2:1 Paul says that on one occasion he 'went up ... to Jerusalem with Barnabas, taking Titus along'. All the relevant evidence points to Antioch as the place from which they went up. Antioch had been evangelized a few years previously, and many Greeks (Gentiles) in the city had been converted to Christianity. Titus himself was a Greek, and probably one of Paul's converts (in Tit. 1:4 he is addressed, like Timothy in 1 Tim. 1:2, as Paul's 'true-born child').

Barnabas and Paul went up to Jerusalem to discuss

with the leaders of the mother-church the demarcation
of the zones of their missionary activity.[1] But why did
they take Titus with them? Since the evangelism of
Gentiles was under discussion, perhaps they judged it
appropriate to have a representative Gentile convert
with them. Luther suggested that Titus was taken
along as a test case, 'to prove that grace was equally
sufficient for Gentiles and Jews, whether in circumcision or without circumcision'.[2] If there were some
members of the Jerusalem church, like those who
found their voice in Acts 15:5, who maintained that
Gentile converts should be circumcised – well, here
was Titus: what was to be done about him?

In the event, says Paul, 'not even Titus, who was
with me, was compelled to be circumcised, Greek
though he was' (Gal. 2:3). As I read the context, Paul
says that on that occasion the question of circumcising
him was not even raised. The circumcision dispute
arose later, when people described by Paul as 'false
brethren smuggled in' infiltrated into the open fellowship at Antioch (cf. Acts 15:1).[3]

But the statement that 'not even Titus … was
compelled to be circumcised' could be understood in
more than one way. The word 'compelled' could be
emphasized so as to imply: 'He was not *compelled*, to be
sure, but the operation was performed voluntarily' –
whether on Titus's own initiative, or on Paul's, would
be a matter of debate. The break in construction
between verse 4 and verse 5 is awkward, and has
provoked suspicion. 'Who can doubt', asked F.C.

---

[1] See p. 20.
[2] In his first lecture-course on Galatians, 1516–17. See F.F. Bruce, *The Epistle to the Galatians* (Paternoster, 1982), pp. 107 f.
[3] Bruce, *The Epistle to the Galatians*, pp. 111–117.

Burkitt, 'that it was the knife which really did circumcise Titus that has cut the syntax of Galatians 2:3–5 to pieces?'[4]

When a rhetorical question is asked in this form – 'who can doubt?' – it is useful if someone replies, '*I can*'. T.W. Manson gave a reply to that effect, though not in those words: 'If he was circumcised, the fact would be well advertised in Galatia by Paul's opponents, and the involved and stumbling verbiage of these verses would be worse than useless as a camouflage for that nasty fact'.[5]

If Titus, a Gentile Christian, had been circumcised, especially with Paul's consent, the pass would have been sold and the battle for gospel liberty lost before it was well joined. The case of Titus was totally different from Timothy's (at which we looked in an earlier chapter).[6]

When Titus next appears, several years have elapsed. He is still in Paul's company, the kind of man whom the apostle could entrust with delicate commissions.

It is evident from the Corinthian correspondence that relations between Paul and the church of Corinth were far from smooth. There was one occasion on which they had become so strained that Paul cancelled a plan to visit Corinth and instead sent the church a letter. He says he wrote it with tears (2 Cor. 2:4), and evidently he used such severe language that, as soon as he had sent it off, he began to be sorry that he had done so. How would the church react? Paul could

---

[4] F.C. Burkitt, *Christian Beginnings* (University of London Press, 1924), p. 118.
[5] T.W. Manson, *Studies in the Gospels and Epistles* (Manchester University Press, 1962), pp. 175 f.
[6] See p. 31.

scarcely wait to find out. He was in the province of
Asia at the time, and sent Titus across the Aegean to
Corinth, with instructions to him to come back and
report as soon as possible. Probably Titus took the
letter with him; if not, he followed hard on its heels. If
Titus returned while the sea was still open, he would
take a ship bound for Troas; if, by the time he set out
on his return journey, navigation had ceased for the
winter (as it did about November 11), he would have
to travel by land, north through Thessaly and Macedonia and then east through Thrace to the Hellespont.

Paul went to Troas in hope that he would meet
Titus there. In Troas there was a wide open field for
missionary activity, but Paul was too unsettled in
mind to take proper advantage of it. (In fact, he quite
probably achieved more than he realized; a year or two
later, as Acts 20:6–12 would indicate, there seems to
have been a Christian community there.) When at last
it became clear that Titus could no longer come by
sea, Paul set out by road, crossing the straits into
Europe and taking the Egnatian Way into Macedonia,
hoping to meet Titus as he travelled north (2 Cor.
1:23–2: 13).

His hope was realized: the news was good. His letter
had been completely effective. When he sent Titus to
Corinth, he told him (hoping against hope, perhaps)
that the Corinthians were loyal at heart. Indeed they
were, Titus reported. There had been a wholesale
revulsion of feeling in Paul's favour. The church was
thoroughly ashamed of its treatment of him and had
disciplined an unnamed member who had apparently
taken the lead in the opposition to him. So severe was
the discipline that Paul wrote to tell them they had
gone far enough: he cherished no personal resentment

against the man and begged the church to forgive him as he himself did.

The Corinthians had certainly vindicated Paul's good account of them; Titus was impressed by them. In fact, he had established friendly relations with them on his own account. He was overjoyed by his reception, as Paul was by his report (2 Cor. 7:6–16).

Paul planned to visit Jerusalem in a few months' time along with delegates of the Gentile churches, taking their contributions for the relief fund which Paul had been organizing for the past year and more. The Corinthians had expressed their interest in this matter at an early stage (1 Cor. 16:1–4), but while relations were strained their keenness probably flagged, and it would not have been politic for Paul to raise the matter with them. But in the present atmosphere of reconciliation he could take it up again, and who better to be his messenger than Titus? So he sent Titus back to Corinth, in the hope that as he had done so well with one work of grace (the mission of reconciliation), so he might be equally successful with another – the grace of generosity (2 Cor. 8:6f.). As monetary matters were too liable to misrepresentation to be handled by one person only, he sent two others with Titus. One was the unnamed 'brother whose praise in the gospel is in all the churches' and who had been selected by the contributing churches themselves as their agent (2 Cor. 8:18f.)[7]; the other was a brother, also unnamed, whose trustworthiness Paul had proved in other commissions and who had great confidence in the Corinthian church. These men, Paul hoped, would be acceptable to the Corinthians and would help them

7 See p. 39.

to complete their contribution to the 'collection for the saints'.

But the outcome was not so happy after all. Paul's opponents in Corinth recovered their second wind. They sowed suspicions about this collection, and about Paul's messengers. Paul was too crafty, they said, to handle their money himself; he sent others to do it for him. Paul had to challenge them to confess that Titus was as completely above-board in the matter as he himself was (2 Cor. 12:16–18). But the tone of 2 Cor. 10–13 is so different from that of 2 Cor. 1–9 as to suggest that the mood of reconciliation did not last long. This second mission to Corinth probably left Titus a sadder but a wiser man; he had not reckoned with the volatile Corinthian temperament.

Apart from a passing reference to his setting out on one occasion for Dalmatia (2 Tim. 4:10), we bid farewell to Titus, so far as the biblical record is concerned, on the island of Crete, where Paul has left him to set things to rights in the churches and in particular to appoint elders 'in city by city' (Tit. 1:5). It is not certain to what phase of Paul's career this Cretan visit should be assigned. Since Paul does not appear to have landed in Crete during his voyage to Italy (Acts 27:7–15), the Cretan mission must be placed either between the end of his Ephesian ministry and his last journey to Jerusalem (according to one writer, he could not have written as he does in Rom. 15:23 about no longer having any room for work in the eastern Mediterranean if Crete had remained unevangelized)[8] or else in the no man's land between his first and second Roman imprisonments.

[8] J.M. Gilchrist, in an unpublished Ph.D. thesis on 'The Authorship and Date of the Pastoral Epistles' (University of Manchester, 1966), p. 189.

But whatever be the precise date of Titus's ministry in Crete, he has not been forgotten there. He is remembered especially at Gortyn, capital city of Crete in Roman times, where the ancient basilica of St. Titus is believed to cover his tomb. It was Titus, a local guide assured us, who first evangelized the island: 'he made a good job of it too; to this day 98 per cent of the people of Crete are Christians.'[9]

Why is there no mention of Titus in Acts? We do not know. There is, for the matter of that, no mention of Luke himself; but that could be due to the author's modesty. Besides, Titus plays a more responsible part in Paul's letters than Luke does, so that his absence from Acts is the more surprising. It has been suggested by some students that Titus and Luke were brothers.[10] This is not impossible: both were Gentiles and both apparently came from Antioch, but more evidence than that would be necessary to establish the relationship. But if Luke was the brother whose 'praise in the gospel' was so widespread and who accompanied Titus to Corinth to help in administering the Jerusalem relief fund, then a blood-relationship can be ruled out. The precise point of his accompanying Titus was that he should be an independent guarantor of the probity of the administration of the money; and this end would have been defeated if critics had been given an opportunity to point to his belonging to the same family as Titus. Such a circumstance would arouse

---

[9] The proportion of Christians was not so high before Crete gained its independence from the Turks in 1898; until then there was a considerable Muslim element in the population of the island.

[10] See A. Souter, 'A Suggested Relationship between Titus and Luke', *Expository Times* 18 (1906–7), p. 285; 'The Relationship between Titus and Luke', *ibid.*, pp. 335 f.

suspicion in that part of the world today as certainly as in the first century.

We must remain ignorant of much that we should like to know; but we can be grateful for what we do know about Titus – a fine example of Christian integrity and responsible service in the circle of Paul's friends.[11]

[11] See also C.K. Barrett, 'Titus', in *Neotestamentica et Semitica: Studies in Honour of Matthew Black*, ed. E.E. Ellis and M. Wilcox (T. & T. Clark, 1969), pp. 1–14.

9

Onesimus of Colossae

Towards the end of his letter to the Colossians Paul tells them that he is sending his friend Tychicus to give them news of him. (Presumably Tychicus, whom we know from Acts 20:4 to have been a native of the province of Asia – possibly of south-western Phrygia, to which Colossae belonged – carried the letter with him.) With Tychicus he sent 'Onesimus, the faithful and beloved brother, who is one of yourselves' (Col. 4:7–9).

If that were the only mention of Onesimus, we should have known that he was a friend of Paul and a member of the church of Colossae: nothing more. But happily we have a further source of information about Onesimus, and from it we can reconstruct a good part of his romantic story. If Tychicus carried the letter to the Colossian church (and perhaps the letter to the Laodicean church as well), Onesimus had also a letter to carry and deliver – a letter that affected him personally. This is the letter to Philemon, the shortest of Paul's letters that have been preserved for us in the New Testament.

Onesimus was a slave in the household of Philemon. Before he himself came to faith with Christ, he must have known something of the gospel: not only was his master a Christian, but he put his house at the disposal of some members at least of the Colossian church for their meetings.

In circumstances of which we are not informed, Onesimus left his master's service. He may simply have seized an opportunity to escape; he may have been sent to fulfil some commission and outstayed his leave, so that he required a note of excuse from Paul begging Philemon's pardon for his unduly long absence. We do not know. Paul hints at the possibility that Onesimus had defrauded his master in some way; if so, he says, he himself will make restitution.

Paul was in custody when Onesimus and he met. Where was he in custody? The traditional account is that he was in Rome, and that is probably right. But arguments have been put forward, notably by the late G.S. Duncan of St. Andrews, for supposing that it was during an Ephesian imprisonment that Paul met Onesimus. Why, it is asked, should Onesimus go so far away as Rome, over a thousand miles from home, when he could easily hide himself in the great city of Ephesus, only a hundred miles away?[1] It is just as likely that Onesimus went to Rome because it was far away as that he went to Ephesus because it was near.[2]

[1] See G.S. Duncan, *St. Paul's Ephesian Ministry* (Hodder & Stoughton, 1929), pp. 72–75.

[2] See C.H. Dodd, 'The Mind of Paul' in *New Testament Studies* (Manchester University Press, 1953), pp. 94–96.

It will be assumed that the situation envisaged belongs to the period of two years that Paul spent under house-arrest in Rome waiting for his appeal to be heard in the imperial court (Acts 28:30).

How did Onesimus make his way to Paul? Again, we do not know. Perhaps Epaphras of Colossae, the evangelist of the Lycus valley, who was on a visit to Paul at the time (Col 1:7, 8; 4:12, 13), came across Onesimus in Rome, recognized him, and brought him to Paul, knowing that Paul would help him in his predicament.

The result of his meeting Paul was that Onesimus became a believer. Not only so, but a warm affection speedily developed between Paul and Onesimus – 'my child Onesimus', says Paul, 'whose father I have become in my imprisonment' (Philem. 10). Paul's movements were restricted, but Onesimus could and did make himself very useful to the apostle by acting as his attendant and messenger. Paul came to value his loving services very highly. Onesimus, of course, could not undertake the kind of responsibilities with which Timothy was entrusted; but Timothy's responsibilities, as we have seen, sometimes took him away for lengthy periods: Onesimus was always available. Paul might have gone on indefinitely availing himself of the help that Onesimus was so willing to give him; but another consideration was in his mind.

Philemon, Onesimus's master, was (like Onesimus himself) one of Paul's converts. He might well cherish a feeling of resentment against Onesimus, and perhaps Onesimus felt something of the same kind against Philemon. There could be no place for a spirit of resentment between the two men who were now brothers in Christ: they must be reconciled. Onesimus must go back to Philemon, and Philemon must forgive Onesimus. When the word 'must' is used in such a context, it is the 'must' of divine constraint from within, not the 'must' of complusion from without. Paul could not compel Philemon to forgive Onesimus; he could not even compel Onesimus to go back to Philemon. But he made it easy for him to go: he gave him a letter to present to Philemon and he arranged that Onesimus should have the company and encouragement of Tychicus as he went. There is no question here of returning a runaway slave to his master. That was what Roman law required,[3] but law does not enter into the picture painted for us in the letter to Philemon. The principals in the situation are fellow-Christians, and the grace of Christ rules in their hearts. Onesimus is returning to Philemon 'no longer as a slave but...as a beloved brother' (Philem. 16).

The delicacy of Paul's approach to Philemon is admirable. He does not tell Philemon what to do – if Philemon decided to retain Onesimus and find him henceforth as useful as his name declared him to be,[4] he was undoubtedly entitled to do so. But Paul suggests that what he would really like Philemon to do was to send Onesimus back to Rome to go on serving Paul as he had begun to do – and when he comes back with your consent, says Paul, he will be serving me on your behalf. You would certainly like to help me, but

---

[3] The law of Israel, on the other hand, manifested in this regard a humanity remarkable for its day: 'You shall not give up to his master a slave who has escaped from his master to you' (Deut. 23:15). Athenian law permitted a slave in danger of his life to seek refuge at an altar: the hearth of a private household was reckoned as an altar for this purpose.

[4] Gk. *onēsimos* means 'profitable'; cf. the verb *oninēmi*, used in the middle voice in Philem. 20, where Paul says to Philemon, 'May I have this profit from you.' See p. 71, n. 5.

such help, of course, should be 'of your own free will' (Philem. 13, 14). The promise to make good any loss that Philemon had incurred through Onesimus, the reminder of the debt that Philemon owed Paul, the indication that Paul may pay Philemon a visit shortly, would all weigh with Philemon. So, probably, would be the mention of Onesimus in the letter to the Colossian church. Onesimus was no doubt known to several members of the church before, but he had not been a member; now, however, as a believer, he could be called 'one of you', as Paul puts it. This meant that the church of Colossae would feel some responsibility for Onesimus's wellbeing.

Was Paul's request granted? If Philemon had re-fused to accept Onesimus as a brother, as Paul's representative, but had treated him with the severity which he felt he deserved, the letter to Philemon would have been suppressed: we should have known nothing of it. But it was not suppressed; it was preserved, and from the earliest formation of the canon of the New Testament its place within the canon has been secure. Since this is one of the things that we have 'received', we tend to take its preservation for granted, ascribing it, and rightly so (in the language of the Westminster Confession), to God's 'singular care and providence'. But the inclusion of this short note in the collection of Pauline letters should make one ask questions, even if the evidence for answering them is almost entirely lacking. Certainly, if only we knew the facts, as interesting a story lies behind the fortunes of this letter after it reached its destination as lies behind its composition in the first instance.

About fifty years after the events surveyed above, Ignatius, bishop of Antioch, was taken under armed guard from Syria to Rome to be martyred in the Colosseum. The journey was broken in Smyrna, where Ignatius was visited by Christian leaders from neighbouring cities, including the bishop of Ephesus, a man named Onesimus. But Onesimus was quite a common name, borne by both slaves and freemen. Is there any reason for connecting the Onesimus who lived in Ephesus about A.D. 110 with the Onesimus about whom Paul wrote to Philemon half a century before?

After the bishop of Ephesus had visited Ignatius, Ignatius sent a letter to the church of Ephesus, thanking the Christians for the kindness they had shown him in the person of their bishop. This letter is one of the few places in early Christian literature where the language of the letter to Philemon is clearly echoed. Ignatius shows himself familiar with the letter to Philemon, particularly in that part of his letter to Ephesus in which specific reference is made to Bishop Onesimus. As Paul plays on the meaning of the name Onesimus when he says to Philemon, 'May I have this "profit" from you' (verse 20), so does Ignatius when he says to the Ephesian church, 'May I always have "profit" from you'.[5]

It could be, of course, that the name of the bishop of Ephesus reminded Ignatius of the earlier Onesimus, so that the phraseology of Paul's letter came unbidden to his lips. As the earlier Onesimus, formerly unprofitable, was henceforth going to be as 'profitable' as his name promised, so the later Onesimus was, as Ignatius said, eminently worthy of his 'well-loved name'. But the identification of the two bearers of the name is not at all impossible. If Paul's Onesimus was in his

---

[5] Ignatius, *To the Ephesians* 2:2, using the same verb as Paul had used (see p. 69, n. 4).

late 'teens or early twenties at the time of his conversion, he would have been about seventy at the time of Ignatius's last journey.

One well-known American school has propounded the view that the first collection of Paul's letters was made in Ephesus about the beginning of the second century; some members of the school have speculated that Bishop Onesimus played a responsible part in the collection and that the letter to Philemon was included because of its personal significance for him.[6] This view has not found widespread acceptance; it has more of fancy than of fact about it. Yet the preservation and canonization of this private letter must be explained. To Paul's Onesimus this letter was his charter of liberty. If indeed it was this Onesimus who became bishop of Ephesus, then, wherever and by whomsoever the first collection of Pauline letters was made, he could scarcely fail to get to know about it, and would make sure that this letter found a place in the collection.

There is so much that we should like to know about Onesimus that he presents a standing invitation to the writer of historical fiction. Authors as diverse as Naomi Mitchison and Patricia St. John have filled in the gaps imaginatively.[7] But, even if we confine ourselves to the few hard facts that we have about Onesimus, his story is of great value because of the light that it throws on the personality of Paul and on his relations with his friends.

---

[6] The Chicago school led by E.J. Goodspeed (1871–1962); see especially J. Knox, *Philemon among the Letters of Paul* (Collins, ²1960).

[7] N. Mitchison, 'The Triumph of Faith' in *When the Bough Breaks* (London: Jonathan Cape, 1927), pp. 91–158; P. St. John, *Twice R₋ıeased* (Pickering & Inglis, 1970).

10

Mark, the cousin of Barnabas

This paper starts with two assumptions. The first is that 'Mark the cousin of Barnabas' from whom Paul sends greetings to the church of Colossae (Col. 4:10), and who is named in two other places in the epistles (Philem. 24; 2 Tim. 4:11), is identical with John Mark of Jerusalem who figures briefly in the Acts of the Apostles (Acts 12:12, etc.). The second is that this Mark is the author of the Second Gospel. The first of these assumptions is a virtual certainty; the second is highly probable. Nothing shall be said here of the suggestion that he was the young man who escaped naked from the scene of Jesus' arrest (Mark 14:51 f.) or that he was the son of the householder who lent his guest-room for the Last Supper (Mark 14:14).[1]

[1] These possibilities are elaborated in J.A. Robertson, *The Hidden Romance of the New Testament* (James Clarke, 1920), pp. 25–63. (The word 'romance' in the title of this work, by a former Aberdeen professor, should be noted.) See p. 77, n. 8.

Mark, as Paul says, was Barnabas's cousin. The AV renders the term differently: 'sister's son to Barnabas', it calls him. This rendering goes back to Tyndale; he in turn may have been influenced by Luther, who calls Mark Barnabas's nephew (*der Neffe des Barnabas*). Before Tyndale, Wycliffe had given the correct rendering 'cousin' (following the Latin *consobrinus*). There is no ambiguity about the Greek word *anepsios*, which Paul uses: 'cousin' – even 'first cousin' – is what it means.[2] The rendering 'nephew' or 'sister's son' may have been due to the impression given in Acts that Mark was substantially younger than Barnabas, who took him under his wing.

Like many Jews of the period (including Paul himself), Mark had two names – a Jewish name, John (*Yohanan* in Hebrew), and a Gentile name, Mark (the very common Roman name *Marcus*). His mother, Mary, owned a house in Jerusalem which served as a meeting place for one group of the primitive church in that city – an influential group, for Peter evidently belonged to it.[3] Since Mark's father is not mentioned as the householder, it may be presumed that he was dead by this time. Mark grew up, then, in close contact with the earliest leaders of the church.

When, about A.D. 46, Barnabas and Paul came to Jerusalem with a monetary gift to the church from the Christians in Syrian Antioch, they probably lodged with Mary, who would have been Barnabas's aunt. Mark was no doubt fascinated by these two visitors, especially (it may be) by his cousin, and when they invited him to accompany them on their return to

---

[2] The Septuagint accurately uses this word of the 'sons of their father's brothers' to whom the daughers of Zelophehad were married (Num. 36:11).
[3] See Acts 12:12.

Antioch he jumped at the opportunity. Next to Rome and Alexandria, Antioch was the largest city in the world: here was a chance to broaden his horizons. But, not long after their arrival in Antioch, a chance to broaden them even farther came his way: Barnabas and Paul were released by the church of Antioch to embark on a wider missionary outreach, and they took Mark with them as their assistant.

Perhaps Mark did not take kindly to the rigours of the itinerant life. He remained with Barnabas and Paul as they travelled through Cyprus from east to west, and he went with them when they set sail from Paphos for the south coast of Asia Minor, but when they came to the river-port of Perga in Pamphylia and proposed to strike up country, he decided he had had enough, and (for whatever reason) took the next ship back to his native land.[4]

A year or two later, Barnabas and Paul thought to set out from Antioch to revisit the churches they had recently planted in Cyprus and Asia Minor, but Paul refused to take Mark along again, as Barnabas wished to do. Since they could not agree about this, they parted company. 'Barnabas took Mark with him and sailed away to Cyprus' (Acts 15:39).[5] It appears that, under his cousin's tutelage, Mark's spiritual development made encouraging progress. Mark may have been the kind of person who always works best in association with a senior partner: in later years we find him thus associated not only with Barnabas but also with Paul and Peter.

The next time Mark is mentioned in the New Testament he is in Rome (if Rome is, as I believe, the

4 See p. 18.
5 See p. 21.

place from which the letters to the Colossians and to
Philemon were sent). Writing to the church of Colossae about A.D. 60, Paul sends greetings from three
fellow-Christians of Jewish birth and three of Gentile
birth. The first three are Aristarchus, Mark and Jesus
Justus.[6] Of these three he says, 'they have been a
comfort to me' (Col. 4:11). Of Mark he says, 'you have
received instructions concerning him; if he comes to
you, give him a welcome' (Col. 4:10). We may wish we
knew something more about this proposed visit by
Mark to the Lycus valley, but no further information is
available. Writing about the same time to Philemon,
Paul again sends greetings from Mark as well as from
other 'fellow-workers'.

It is plain that Mark has completely rehabilitated
himself in Paul's good opinion, and this may well have
been due to the helping hand he received from Barnabas at a time when he was tempted to think himself
useless so far as any further Christian service was
concerned. Paul's last reference to Mark comes in 2
Tim. 4:11 where, urging Timothy to come and rejoin
him soon, he adds, 'Take Mark and bring him with
you, for he is very useful to me for ministry.' The
Dutch jurist Hugo Grotius in the seventeenth century
thought that the particular usefulness Paul had in
mind was Mark's fluency in Latin; that is as it may be.
(There is no evidence that Mark was specially fluent in
Latin; in Rome at that time one could get by very well
with Greek.)

But Paul was not the only Christian leader to find
Mark very useful for ministry. When, in 1 Pet. 5:13,
greetings are sent to the readers of that letter from 'my

---

[6] On Aristarchus and Jesus Justus see pp. 35, 86.

son Mark', we may have New Testament confirmation
for the tradition which makes Mark aide-de-camp to
the apostle Peter. This tradition appears to be based
on a statement in the writings of Papias, who about
A.D. 130 was bishop of Hierapolis in the Lycus valley:

> Mark became Peter's interpreter and wrote down accur-
> ately, although not in order, all that he [Peter] men-
> tioned of the sayings or doings of the Lord. Mark had
> never heard the Lord or accompanied him, but later (as I
> said) he accompanied Peter, who composed his teaching
> as the needs of the occasion required, not as though he
> were making a systematic arrangement of the Lord's
> oracles. Mark, then, made no mistake in thus writing
> points down one by one as he [Peter] remembered them;
> for he paid attention to this one thing – to leave out
> nothing of what he heard and include no false statement
> among them.[7]

It is uncertain if Papias said anything more about
Mark. His writings have been lost, apart from isolated
quotations preserved by other authors: the paragraph
just reproduced was quoted by Eusebius. Another
document which is probably dependent on Papias is
the so-called anti-Marcionite prologue to the Gospel of
Mark, which says that Mark was nicknamed 'stump-
fingered' (Gk. *kolobodaktylos*)[8] and that 'after Peter's
departure he committed his Gospel to writing in the
parts of Italy'.

If we try, with due caution, to reconstruct the
historical situation behind this tradition, we might

[7] This extract from Papias's lost *Exegesis of the Dominical Logia* (compiled about
A.D. 125) is preserved in Eusebius, *Ecclesiastical History* 3.39.15.
[8] The origin of this nickname is unknown; several guesses have been made about
it, including that of the author of this prologue (or his source), that Mark's fingers
were short in proportion to the rest of his body. Other guesses have been more
imaginative, such as that he had his finger-tips sliced off when he ran away naked
from the men who tried to seize him at Jesus' arrest (J.A. Robertson, *The Hidden
Romance of the New Testament*, p. 35). See p. 73, n. 1.

envisage a visit paid to Italy by Peter and Mark in the later 50s of the first century.[9] It appears from 1 Corinthians that, from about mid-century onward, Peter embarked on a more extended ministry than he had exercised until then. If he continued to respect the agreement which he and his colleagues had reached with Paul and Barnabas in Jerusalem (Gal. 2:7–9) and concentrated on the mission to the Jews, he would find plenty of scope for such a mission in the Mediterranean provinces: in Rome itself there may have been as many Jews as there were in Jerusalem. Nor would he forget that he had been commissioned not only to be a fisher of men but also to care for the Lord's flock. With Claudius's death and Nero's accession the edict banning Jews from Rome (issued in A.D. 49) would have become a dead letter: among the Jews who flooded back to the capital were many followers of Jesus, and a visit from Peter was just what was needed to establish them in faith and witness. Mark would have served him well as interpreter and in other ways.

After his visit to Rome, Peter moved elsewhere, but Mark stayed on. He was there when Paul arrived in the city at the beginning of A.D. 60, and he sought him out in his lodgings for old time's sake. Neither Mark nor Paul would have let an ancient misunderstanding stand in the way of friendship and fellowship, and indeed Mark found ways of bringing help and comfort to Paul in his restricted circumstances. It is uncertain if Mark was able to carry out the visit to Asia Minor which Paul mentions as a possibility in Col. 4:10. If he did, he most probably returned to Rome, for it is a

---

[9] See G. Edmundson, *The Church of Rome in the First Century* (Longmans, 1913), pp. 80, 84; T.W. Manson, *Studies in the Gospels and Epistles* (Manchester University Press, 1962), pp. 38–45.

near-certainty that it was in Rome or its vicinity that
he produced his Gospel, thus initiating a new literary
genre:

> The saint who first found grace to pen
> The life which was the Life of men.[10]

He appears to have produced it not simply to
provide Peter's hearers in Rome with a written record
of what the apostle had told them during his visit.
While there are features in the Gospel which reflect
Peter's oral narrative, its central emphases suggest
that it was composed as 'a call to Christian loyalty and
a challenge to a hostile world' (C.H. Dodd) soon after
Nero's murderous attack on the Christians of Rome
which followed the great fire of A.D. 64. Nothing was
better calculated to restore their morale and their
sense of identity than this little book, which contained
the community's own account of its origin and, in
particular, reminded them how their Lord had emphasized that those who wished to be his disciples must
follow him in the way of the cross, drinking his cup
and sharing his baptism.[11]

A later tradition credits Mark with the foundation of
the church of Alexandria in Egypt. But Alexandrian
Christianity certainly antedates the period at which
Mark might be expected to engage in such activity.
There may be nothing more behind the tradition than
the arrival at Alexandria of an early copy of the Gospel
of Mark, sent from Rome.[12] If it has any further basis,

[10] Laurence Housman.
[11] C.H. Dodd, *About the Gospels* (Cambridge University Press, 1950), p. 2.
[12] See C.H. Roberts, 'The Christian Book and the Greek Papyri', *Journal of Theological Studies* 50 (1949), pp. 155–168; L.W. Barnard, 'St. Mark and Alexandria', *Harvard Theological Review* 57 (1964), pp. 145–150. The tradition associating Mark with the foundation of Alexandrian Christianity is preserved in Eusebius, *Ecclesiastical History* 2.16.1.

it may lie in a second-century attempt to reconstitute the Christian community in Alexandria as a daughter-church of Rome, and to provide it with an orthodox and near-apostolic pedigree. There could no no question of Rome's sharing *Peter* with the church of Alexandria, but Mark, Peter's junior colleague, would serve very well. So Mark was awarded this posthumous distinction.

But his reputation is securely enough established to dispense with such doubtful aid as this. Mark the Evangelist has left an imperishable legacy to all succeeding generations. And, as a member of three intersecting circles in the early church, he provides an important link between Barnabas, Peter and Paul.

11

Paul's Co-Workers

There is a frequently quoted passage in one of T.R. Glover's books where he speaks of the apostle's fondness for words compounded with the prefix *syn* (meaning 'with'). These compounds, according to Glover, have two main functions: one, to emphasize Paul's union with the crucified and risen Christ, and the other, to emphasize his fellowship with other Christians, especially those actively engaged in propagating the gospel.[1]

One of the most frequent of those compounds in Paul's vocabulary is the noun *synergos*, 'co-worker' or 'fellow-worker'. 'To a man or woman of any spirit or character', say Glover, 'to be so described by one of Paul's build and nature must have been in itself inspiration.'[2]

[1] T.R. Glover, *Paul of Tarsus* (SCM Press, 1925), pp. 178–183.
[2] *Paul of Tarsus*, pp. 178 f.

Some of the people whom Paul describes as his 'co-workers' have been treated in previous chapters in this book – Prisca and Aquila, for example (Rom. 16:3), Timothy (Rom. 16:21), Titus (2 Cor. 8:23), Mark (Col. 4:10; Philem. 24) and Luke (Philem. 24). But there are other 'co-workers' of whom we know less.

There is Aristarchus, for example, called a co-worker in Col. 4:10 and Philem. 24. In Col. 4:10 he is also called Paul's *synaichmalōtos*, his 'fellow-prisoner' (literally, 'fellow-prisoner-of-war'). According to Luke, he was a Macedonian Christian, from Thessalonica; he was with Paul in Ephesus, joined him later on his last journey to Jerusalem, and joined him yet again when he set out on his voyage from Judaea to Italy (Acts 19:29; 20:4; 27:2). Sir William Ramsay suggested that on his voyage Luke and Aristarchus 'must have gone' as Paul's slaves, being actually registered as such on the passenger list.[3] It seems much more likely to me that Luke signed on as ship's doctor, but Ramsay could be right about Aristarchus: we just don't know. Luke, at an earlier stage, calls Aristarchus one of Paul's 'fellow-travellers' (Acts 19:29); if Paul himself calls him a fellow-prisoner, that may mean that he was currently sharing his confinement in Rome, or that he had done so in Ephesus or Caesarea.

But there are others to whom Paul refers as his 'fellow-prisoners'. One of these is Epaphras (Philem. 23). Epaphras, whom he calls his 'fellow-slave' (*syndoulos*) in Col. 1:7, was evidently the evangelist of the Lycus valley and had a pastoral concern for the churches planted there – Colossae, Hierapolis and

---

[3] W.M. Ramsay, *St. Paul the Traveiler and the Roman Citizen* (Hodder & Stoughton, [14]1920), p. 316

Laodicea (Col. 4:13). Even when he was with Paul as his fellow-prisoner, and unable to visit those churches, he prayed hard for them all the time – obviously another man after Paul's own heart.

At an earlier date two other 'fellow-prisoners' are mentioned – Andronicus and Junia,[4] Jewish believers whose faith in Christ antedated Paul's. 'They are of note among the apostles', Paul adds (Rom. 16:7), meaning that they were not only known *to* the apostles but eminent apostles themselves, possibly because they were witnesses of Christ in resurrection. They were resident in Rome when Paul sent his letter to the Christians there; we can only guess at the circumstances in which they had been Paul's fellow-prisoners (perhaps in Ephesus).

To return to others whom Paul calls his 'co-workers', there is Philemon of Colossae, mentioned already in our chapter on Onesimus.[5] A curious thing – is it not? – that nearly two thousand years later the slave rather than the master should receive a study to himself in a series like this! Paul addresses Philemon as 'our beloved fellow-worker' (Philem. 1) and expresses appreciation of all Philemon's activities, not least in the provision of hospitality to fellow-Christians. To see such evident signs of grace in one of his converts was meat and drink to Paul. With Philemon he couples Apphia, presumably his wife, and he salutes another member of the household, Archippus, possibly their

---

[4] It is impossible to tell from the Greek form used here whether the name was Junia (feminine) or Junias (masculine). But the name Junias (or Junianus, of which it would be an abbreviation) does not appear to occur elsewhere. In his commentary on *Romans* (1975–79), p. 788, C.E.B. Cranfield says, 'it is surely right to assume that the person referred to was a woman. ... Most probably Andronicus and Junia were husband and wife.' I agree.

[5] See p. 67.

son. Archippus was also a co-worker, although Paul calls him rather 'co-fighter' (*synstratiōtēs*) – 'our fellow-soldier' (Philem. 2). In Col. 4:17 the Christians of Colossae are directed to convey a message to Archippus: 'See that you fulfil the ministry which you have received in the Lord.' Had Archippus been present when the letter was delivered and read in the church, it would not have been necessary to convey the message to him indirectly; possibly he had been seconded for service in another church (Laodicea has been surmised). But the Colossians knew, and Archippus knew, what the ministry was; they were not left to guess, as we are.

There is another man whom Paul calls his 'fellow-soldier': he is Epaphroditus of Philippi – 'my brother and fellow-worker and fellow-soldier' (Phil. 2:25). Epaphroditus was entrusted by the members of the Philippian church with a gift of money for Paul, who was under house-arrest in Rome (Phil. 4:18). They asked him further, when he came to Paul, to give him what help he could as their representative. But at some point in the discharge of his commission, Epaphroditus fell ill and nearly died. News of his illness got back to Philippi and filled his friends there with anxiety; he knew that they had heard of it and was himself anxious to relieve their fears, but at the same time he was anxious to stay on in Rome and make himself useful to Paul. But Paul sent him back with a letter in which he not only thanks the Philippian Christians for their gift but explains that he takes sole responsibility for Epaphroditus's return to them. If they asked Epaphroditus why he did not stay with Paul and serve him as he had been instructed to do, here was their answer. At the same time Paul expresses deep appreciation of what Epaphroditus has done for him already, and tells the Philippians that this is the kind of man they should honour. The church of Philippi was well supplied with administrators – 'bishops and deacons' (Phil. 1:1) – but if the occasion arose to add to their number, Epaphroditus should not be overlooked. The mind of Christ, which has been eloquently celebrated earlier (in Phil. 2:5–11), was worthily reproduced in Epaphroditus.

Paul had other co-workers in the Philippian church. One of them, Clement, is named in Phil. 4:3, but others – 'the rest of my fellow-workers' – are unnamed. However, their names, says Paul, 'are in the book of life', although they are not in the letter to the Philippians. But the reference to Clement is preceded by honourable mention of two women, Euodia and Syntyche, who, says Paul, 'laboured side by side with me in the gospel'. The verb he uses is quite a strong one (*synathleō*); he uses it earlier in the letter when he speaks of all the Philippian Christians as '*striving side by side* for the faith of the gospel' (Phil. 1:27). Whatever form these two women's collaboration with Paul in his gospel ministry may have taken, it was not confined to making tea for him and his circle – or whatever the first-century counterpart to that activity was. (Euodia and Syntyche are more often remembered for their failure to agree on some matter. It is difficult to agree with others all the time; what would Paul's response have been on an earlier occasion if someone had sent an exhortation: 'I entreat Paul, and I entreat Barnabas, that they be of one mind in the Lord'?)[6]

As for the 'true yokefellow' who is asked to help Euodia and Syntyche, we have already mentioned the

[6] See Gal. 2:13; Acts 15:36–39. Cf. p. 20f. above.

possibility that this may have been Luke, but other suggestions have been made.[7]

But the list of co-workers is not exhausted. In Rom. 16:9 Paul sends greetings to 'Urbanus, our fellow-worker in Christ'. Urbanus bears a name that links him with the city (Latin *urbs*) of Rome, where he evidently resided, but it was apparently in some other place that Paul had come to know and value him as a co-worker.

Then, among the co-workers who were with Paul when the letters to the Colossian church and Philemon were being written, there are some who call for more attention. There was Jesus surnamed Justus, who is mentioned along with Aristarchus and Mark as one of the three co-workers of Jewish birth who were in Paul's company at the time and who had been a 'comfort' to him (Col. 4:11). Like a number of other Jews who we meet in the New Testament, he has both a Jewish name, Jesus (Joshua or Jeshua), and a Gentile (Latin) name, Justus. Of him no more is known than what Paul says of him to the Colossians. Then there was Demas, one of Paul's co-workers of Gentile birth (Col. 4:14; Philem. 24). His name is a shortened form of Demetrius, Demosthenes or Democritus. But Demas is best remembered not as one of Paul's co-workers but as the man who later deserted him 'for love of this present age' (2 Tim. 4:10). An eccentric interpretation of Demas's action was voiced by James Butler Stoney, who held that Demas left Paul in order to conduct an evangelistic campaign in Thessalonica, his love for the 'age' or 'world' being evidently a love for the souls of its pagan population.[8]

[7] See pp. 39, 95.
[8] Cf. W.B. Neatby, *A History of the Plymouth Brethren* (Hodder & Stoughton, 1901), p. 321.

But in that case Paul would not have used a severe verb which means that Demas left him the lurch, or given the strong impression that Demas's love for 'the present age' was of an unworthy kind.[9]

One further colleague is mentioned by Paul towards the end of the letter to Colossae – Tychicus, who was apparently the bearer of that letter (Col. 4:7) and at the same time of the letter to the Ephesians (Eph. 6:21). To the recipients of both these letters he was to bring the latest news of Paul. Paul describes him as 'our dear brother and a trusty servant' (i.e. a trusty servant of Christ) – in fact, as his own 'fellow-slave' in the Lord (using the same word as was used of Epaphras in Col. 1:7). Tychicus was himself a native of the province of Asia, as we learn from Acts 20:4, where he is listed among Paul's fellow-travellers on his last journey to Jerusalem. The evidence of Paul's letters indicates that those fellow-travellers were delegates from their respective Gentile churches, carrying contributions for the church in Jerusalem, so Tychicus was probably commissioned on that occasion to carry the contributions from one or more of the churches of Asia.[10] He is mentioned also on two occasions in the Pastoral Epistles as a messenger of Paul (2 Tim. 4:12; Tit. 3:12).

Paul mentions many other friends whom he does not explicitly call co-workers but from whom he certainly would not have withheld the designation.

The last chapter of the letter to the Romans contains the names of several such people, over and above those whom we have already mentioned. There was Tertius,

---

[9] Those who, without carefully examining the evidence, declare that the verb *agapaō* in itself denotes a noble and self-sacrificing love might ponder the fact that this is the verb used for Demas's love of 'the present age'.
[10] See p. 98.

for example, who co-operated with Paul by taking down the letter at his dictation; he sends his Christian greetings to the recipients in the first person singular (Rom. 16:22). Erastus, the city treasurer of Corinth, and 'our brother Quartus', named almost immediately after Tertius's salutation (Romans 16:23b), were probably also co-workers. Erastus perhaps made good as city treasurer; we find him later occupying a higher position in the civic administration – the position of aedile (curator of public works).[11]

If Tertius, Paul's amanuensis, may properly be called one of his co-workers, so also may Phoebe, who carried the letter to Rome – nearly a four-weeks journey, whichever way she went. Two further pieces of information are given about her: she was a servant (minister or deacon[12]) of the church of Cenchreae (presumably a daughter-church of the metropolitan church of Corinth, situated near the city's Aegean harbour), and she was 'a helper of many' – 'and of myself as well', Paul adds. The word translated 'helper' (*prostatis*, 'patroness') occurs here only in the New Testament; it is related to the verb rendered 'gives aid' in Rom. 12:8. It implies that she was in a position of some affluence or influence, in which she was able to render material aid to others, including Paul himself. If he refused to accept financial support from the Corinthian church, he obviously appreciated the kind

---

[11] Excavations in Roman Corinth in 1929 uncovered a marble pavement, bearing the inscription: 'Erastus, to mark his aedileship, laid this pavement at his own expense'. If this is the same Erastus, it might be argued that his Christian profession led to his demotion from the aedileship to the inferior position of city treasurer. But the pavement appears to be later in date than the letter to the Romans.

[12] She should not be called a 'deaconess', because that too often implies an inferior status to 'deacon'. The Greek word (*diakonos*) may be either masculine or feminine.

of help that Phoebe supplied. She may have been on the point of making a business trip to Rome; Paul commends her to the fellowship and hospitality of her fellow-Christians there (Rom. 16:1 f.).

Again, if Tryphaena and Tryphosa (who, to judge by their names, may have been twin sisters) were 'workers in the Lord', they served the same Master as Paul served, and were therefore co-workers of his in some sense, together with 'the beloved Persis, who has worked hard in the Lord' (Rom. 16:12). The same may be said of that Mary who 'worked hard' among the Christians of Rome (Rom. 16:6). These women are otherwise unknown to us. Their record is on high, no doubt, but it is also preserved, if concisely, on earth.

Finally, there is a man named Onesiphorus, whose help meant much to Paul when he needed it most. He is mentioned twice only – both times in one of the Pastoral Epistles (2 Tim. 1:16–18; 4:19) – but the little that is said of him is eloquent enough. His name is quite like that of Onesimus – it means 'profit-bearing' or 'profit-yielding' – and Paul proved him to be true to his name. He rendered Paul great help in Ephesus (evidently his home city) – by contrast with 'Alexander the coppersmith', who did him 'great harm' (2 Tim.4:14 f.) – and in times of trouble, says Paul, 'he often refreshed me; he was not ashamed of my chains, but when he arrived in Rome he searched for me eagerly and found me.' The imprisonment to which Paul refers here perhaps involved greater restriction than the house-arrest under which he lived for two years (Acts 28:30); it may have been not only difficult to find the apostle but dangerous to be recognized as one of his friends. Was it because of the danger of being publicly associated with him that, as he wrote, 'at my first defence no one took my part; all deserted me' (2 Tim. 4:16)? All the more, then, would he have appreciated the courage and determination shown by Onesiphorus. One writer has drawn a vivid and moving picture of 'one purposeful face in a drifting crowd' as 'this stranger from far coasts of the Aegean ... threads the maze of unfamiliar streets, knocking at many doors, following up every clue, warned of the risks he is taking but not to be turned from his quest; till in some obscure prison-house a known voice greets him, and he discovers Paul chained to a Roman soldier.'[13]

Plainly, too, Onesiphorus had the active support of his family as he went out of his way to be of service to Paul. No wonder that Paul bespeaks the mercy of God on Onesiphorus and his household both in their earthly life and at the great day.[14]

The men and women mentioned, and others un-mentioned, must have esteemed it a great honour to be Paul's fellow-workers in the highest of all enterprises. And Paul, for his part, was warmly appreciative of their fellowship and collaboration. They ministered comfort to him and strengthened his hands in the Lord. One can well believe that, without their self-denying aid, his own ministry would have been much less effective than it was.[15]

---

[13] P.N. Harrison, *The Problem of the Pastoral Epistles* (Oxford University Press, 1921), p. 127.

[14] Onesiphorus evidently made an impression on the presbyter of Asia who, about A.D. 160, wrote a historical novel on the apostle (the *Acts of Paul*); however, he makes him a resident not of Ephesus but of Iconium, where, with his wife Lectra and their children Simmias and Zeno, he entertains Paul.

[15] See E.E. Ellis, 'Paul and his Co-Workers', *New Testament Studies* 17 (1970–71), pp. 437–452, reprinted in his *Prophecy and Hermeneutic in Early Christianity* (Eerdmans, 1978), pp. 3–22.

12

Hosts and Hostesses

Anyone who travelled as much as Paul did was indebted to a wide variety of people for hospitality. If he wanted a roof over his head for the night and a bed of sorts to lie down on, he could usually find an inn, and Paul was happy to pay his way. But inns were dangerous and unsavoury places, and it was better if he could stay in private homes. As the number of his friends and converts increased in one city after another, he could expect to be invited by them to accept their hospitality. But when he visited a city where he knew nobody, he had to make do with such accommodation as was available. When he came to Rome, he stayed in private lodgings; this seems clear whether we accept the rendering 'in his own hired dwelling' or 'at his own expense' in Acts 28:30. It had to be a place where he could conveniently be kept under military surveillance.

Paul's first host whose name is recorded was a man named Judas, who lived in Damascus, in the 'street called Straight' (Acts 9:11) – the street whose name survives in today's Darb al-Mustaqim. We should expect that a room had been booked for him in advance in Judas's house. If an investigative journalist had been around to get to the bottom of Paul's strange experience as he approached Damascus, he would certainly have made a point of interviewing Judas and getting the story from his angle. Judas's account would have been most interesting, but it does not exist. He was probably quite bewildered by the difference between the guest whom he found on his hands and the guest whom he had been led to expect – it was the same man, indeed, but not the same *kind* of man.

We do not know whether Paul continued to stay with Judas during the 'several days' that he was 'with the disciples at Damascus' or if he moved elsewhere. Judas disappears from the record.

The next person to be mentioned as Paul's host is a man whom we know very well. Three years (or in the third year) after his conversion Paul, as he himself tells us, 'went up to Jerusalem to visit Cephas, and remained with him fifteen days' (Gal. 1:18). The implication is that he stayed with Cephas/Peter as his guest. The subsequent story of Paul's relations with Peter is one marked by ups and downs; but their first meeting was evidently a happy one. A record of their conversation during these fifteen days would be illuminating: in a frequently quoted remark of C.H. Dodd, 'we may presume they did not spend all the time talking about the weather'.[1] That they compared notes

---

[1] C.H. Dodd, *The Apostolic Preaching and its Developments* (Hodder & Stoughton, [2]1944), p. 16.

on the risen Lord's earlier appearance to Peter and his later appearance to Paul is certain, and when, during those days, Paul had an opportunity of meeting James, the Lord's brother, James would be able to add his testimony of how the Lord appeared also to him (cf. 1 Cor. 15:5,7,8).

We are not told with whom Paul stayed on his later visits to Jerusalem; on one of them, as has been suggested in an earlier chapter, he and Barnabas perhaps stayed with Mary, the mother of Mark.

There is a noteworthy development in the relation between Paul and Peter in the autobiographical narrative of Gal. 1:11–2: 14. At their first meeting Paul was Peter's guest; at their second meeting (again in Jerusalem) he conferred with him as his fellow-apostle; at their third meeting (in Antioch this time) he 'opposed him to his face, because he stood condemned' (Gal. 2.11).

When Barnabas fetched Paul from Tarsus to join him at Antioch, we do not know with whom Paul stayed at Antioch. But I will make three guesses. First, he stayed with the parents of Rufus, to whom greetings are later sent in Rom. 16:13; it was at that time that Rufus's mother proved herself a mother to Paul. Second, Rufus's mother was the wife of 'Symeon who was called Niger', prophet and teacher in the church of Antioch (Acts 13:1). Third, this man was identical with 'Simon of Cyrene, the father of Alexander and Rufus', to whom we are introduced in Mark 15:21.[2]

---

[2] When Mark introduces Simon of Cyrene into his passion narrative, he says in effect to his readers – in the first instance, I believe, the Christians in Rome (see p. 79) – 'You will know the man I mean when I tell you he was the father of Alexander and Rufus', implying that Alexander and Rufus were known to them. Paul gives us a Rufus who was known to the Roman Christians. One of my students once asked me (referring to the meaning of Rufus's name), 'Would a dark-skinned man have a red-haired son?' – to which I replied, 'His mother was auburn.' (That was a fourth guess!)

Some of these guesses are not entirely without foundation, but guesses they remain.

We have something better than guesswork to guide
us when Paul comes to Philippi. There his first convert
(or one of the first) was Lydia, from Thyatira in the
province of Asia, who traded in the purple ware for
which her native region had been renowned for centur-
ies. The purple dye was derived at this time from the
juice of the madder root. Lydia was a God-fearing
Gentile: since there was a Jewish community in
Thyatira, it may have been in the synagogue there that
she learned to worship the true God. In Philippi there
were probably not sufficient male Jews to constitute a
proper synagogue, so Lydia and some like-minded
women met each sabbath day by the river side, outside
the city, to say the appointed prayers. There Paul and
his companions (Silas, Luke and Timothy) found
them and told them the good news which they were
commissioned to make known. Lydia believed the
message, was baptized with her household (perhaps
her servants rather than her children), and invited the
missionaries, if they reckoned that she was a true
believer, to come and stay in her house. Lydia's house
thus became their headquarters during their time in
Philippi, and it was perhaps (to begin with, at least)
the headquarters of the infant church in the city – it
was apparently in Lydia's house that the missionaries,
before their departure, saw the brethren and encouraged them (Acts 16:14–40).

Lydia appears no more by name in the New Testament. Some have held that Lydia (meaning 'the
Lydian woman') was not her personal name, and that
she should be identified with either Euodia or Syntyche – Paul's two female co-workers who are men-

tioned in Phil. 4:2,3. Others think she was the 'true yoke-fellow' who is addressed directly in that same context. A few – most notably Sabine Baring Gould (author of *Onward, Christian soldiers*) – have suggested that she was Paul's yokefellow not just in the sense of 'co-worker' but in the sense of 'wife'.[3] But, apart from the general improbability of this idea, there is a grammatical objection to it.[4] The idea belongs to the realm of romantic fiction, not of sober history.

There was another person in Philippi whose hospitality Paul enjoyed for a few hours during his first visit to the city. That was the city jailer. I am not thinking of the uncomfortable hours that Paul and Silas spent with their legs fastened in the stocks in the inner prison, where the jailer had locked them up for greater security, but of what happened after the earthquake and the jailer's eager acceptance of the message of salvation. 'He took them the same hour of the night, and washed their wounds, and he was baptized at once, with all his family' (Acts 16:33). As Chrysostom puts it in his homily on the passage, 'he washed and was washed – he washed them from their stripes, and he himself was washed from his sins.' 'Then', as Luke continues the story, 'he brought them up into his house, and set food before them, and believing in God he rejoiced with all his family' (Acts 16:34). No doubt Paul and Silas felt that the indignity, pain and discomfort of the preceding hours was a price well worth paying for the joy of these hours that followed.

---

[3] S. Baring Gould, *A Study of St. Paul* (London: Isbister, 1897), pp. 213–216. This interpretation of Phil. 4:3 commended itself earlier to Clement of Alexandria, Erasmus and Ernest Renan.
[4] While *syzygos* ('yokefellow') may be either masculine or feminine, the form of the adjective *gnēsios* ('true') which qualifies it is masculine.

From Philippi the missionary party (without Luke) moved to Thessalonica, and there they were entertained by a householder named Jason – probably a man of Jewish birth whose native name had been hellenized. Jason found that being host to Paul and his friends exposed him to grave danger. When the local opponents of the gospel engineered a demonstration against the missionaries, Jason's house was attacked and he, with some other converts, was dragged before the city magistrates and charged with harbouring subversive characters, who had come to Thessalonica to urge people to transfer their allegiance from Caesar to a rival ruler. This was a serious charge, but the magistrates kept their heads and contented themselves with requiring Jason and the others to go bail for the missionaries' good behaviour – which meant, in effect, their quiet and prompt departure from the city (Acts 17:5–9). Paul and Silas, accordingly, were sent away by night to Beroea. Among the 'noble' members of the Beroean synagogue they seem to have received hospitality during their stay there, but their stay in Beroea was short: it was essential that Paul, in particular, should be got away quickly for his own safety (Acts 17:10–14).

A few weeks later, Paul arrived in Corinth, where he remained for eighteen months. There his first host and hostess were Aquila and Priscilla, for he is said not only to have worked with them but also 'stayed with them' (Acts 18:3). He probably stayed with them for the whole period of eighteen months, and when, after a brief visit to Judaea and Syria, he settled in Ephesus, it is most likely that he stayed with them there too, for at the end of his Corinthian ministry they moved from Corinth to Ephesus.

But on a later visit to Corinth Paul found another host; by this time Priscilla and Aquila were no longer in residence there. But his new host was an old friend, Gaius by name. Gaius, in fact, was one of Paul's earliest converts in Corinth, one whom he himself baptized (1 Cor. 1:14). When, sending his letter to the Roman Christians from Corinth, Paul conveys greetings from Gaius, he speaks of him as 'host to me and to the whole church' (Rom. 16:23). If Gaius was host to the whole church of Corinth, he must have had an unusally capacious house and was most probably a well-to-do citizen of Corinth. To be a citizen of Corinth implied a special status: Corinth was not an ordinary Greek city but a Roman colony, so its citizens were at the same time Roman citizens. Gaius was one of the eighteen possible forenames (*praenomina*) which a Roman citizen might bear; in addition to his forename he had a second or family name (usually ending in *-ius*) and a third name (*cognomen*). (The pattern may be illustrated by the threefold name of the most famous Gaius of them all: Gaius Julius Caesar.) If Paul's host was indeed a Roman citizen, then his family name and *cognomen* may have been preserved elsewhere in the New Testament. In Acts 18:7 it is said that, when Paul was no longer permitted to use the synagogue of Corinth as his base of operations, a God-fearer named Titius Justus, who lived next door to the synagogue, placed his house at Paul's disposal. A plausible case can be made out for identifying the Gaius of Rom. 16:23 with the Titius Justus of Acts 18:7. By calling him a God-fearer Luke indicates that he was a Gentile who habitually attended the synagogue: Gaius Titius Justus would have been a good Roman name, such as a citizen of Corinth might bear.

When Paul sent his letter to the Romans from the house of Gaius, he was about to set out on his last journey to Jerusalem. With him went delegates from a number of Gentile churches, carrying their churches' contributions to the Jerusalem relief fund. The names of seven of them are listed in Acts 20:4.

Of the seven, Timothy, Aristarchus and Tychicus have been mentioned already in these pages. The others are Sopater (from Beroea), Secundus (a Thessalonian, like Aristarchus), another Gaius (from Derbe[5]) and Trophimus (from Ephesus). Trophimus was the innocent cause of the riot in Jerusalem that led to Paul's arrest and imprisonment, when the rumour spread through the city that Paul had violated the sanctity of the temple by taking this Gentile within the forbidden bounds.[6] Three of the seven – Timothy, Aristarchus and Sopater (if he is identical with the Sosipater of Rom.16:21)[7] – belonged to the circumcision; the rest were evidently Gentile Christians, and there may have been other delegates whose names are not listed.

Not every member of the Jerusalem church would have been happy to offer hospitality to uncircumcised Gentiles, fellow-Christians though they might be – or, for the matter of that, even to Paul himself. It was prudent to arrange hospitality for the party in advance, and arrangement was duly made, perhaps by

[5] The 'western' text says he came not from Derbe but from Doberus, a city of Macedonia. But this is probably an attempt to identify him with the Gaius who, with Aristarchus, was dragged into the theatre at Ephesus on the occasion of the great riot (Acts 19:29). In the majority of manuscripts both Gaius and Aristarchus are there called 'Macedonians'; even so, there is some reason to read the singular, 'a Macedonian', referring to Aristarchus only (in which case the Gaius of Acts 19:29 could still be the same man as the Gaius of Acts 20:4).
[6] Acts 21:27–36.
[7] Paul there includes Sosipater among a group of his 'kinsmen'.

members of the church of Caesarea. For, when the party set out on the last lap of the journey to Jerusalem, 'some of the disciples from Caesarea went with us,' says Luke, 'bringing us to the house of Mnason of Cyprus, an early disciple, with whom we were to lodge' (Acts 21:16). 'An early disciple' means an original disciple: the Greek adjective is *archaios*, implying that Mnason had been a disciple from the beginning (*archē*), a foundation-member of the mother church. He was, like Barnabas, a Cypriot. In fact, he appears to have been one of the few Hellenists left in the church of Jerusalem after the persecution which broke out on the morrow of Stephen's death: most of the believing Hellenists were dispersed at that time and carried the gospel wherever they went. But Mnason (whose name may be a hellenized form of Manasseh) shared the liberal sympathies of those other Hellenists, and it was a pleasure for him to act as host to Gentile believers, with all the inconvenience, disapproval and possible danger in which his hospitality might involve him. Moreover, like Jason and Gaius and others, he could not have been so efficient a host had he not had at his side someone willing to play her part as hostess. Even when the wives of the hosts are not named, their essential role cannot be overlooked.

The last host to be mentioned is a *potential* host: Philemon of Colossae. 'Get a guest room ready for me', says Paul, when writing to Philemon about Onesimus; 'I am hoping through your prayers to be granted to you' (Philem. 22). We do not know if Paul was able to carry out his planned visit to Colossae, but if he was, no doubt Apphia made sure that everything necessary was done for the entertaining of so honoured a guest.

These friends and co-workers, hosts and hostesses,

had no other motive in being so helpful than love of
Paul and love of the Master whom he served. They
knew that in serving the one they were serving the
other. The last thing they thought of was that their
names would be put on perpetual record; indeed, that
was the last thing that Paul himself thought of with
regard to his own name. But he recorded his gratitude
to them all, and their memory lives on – not only in the
pages of the New Testament but in the Christian
names borne by so many people ever since in all parts
of the world. Lydia, Priscilla, Phoebe and Persis;
Mark, Luke, Timothy and Titus – why are these
names still in such widespread use? Because certain
people who bore these names in the first century A.D.
were friends of Paul, and he set down his appreciation
of them in letters that he wrote, and his letters have the
salt of immortality in them. So we read his letters, and
the faith and kindness of those friends of his are
remembered afresh, and their example remains
powerful.

INDEX

INDEX

Achaicus, 56
Acilius Glabrio, 46
Acts of the Apostles, 23, 26, 28, 33, 36
ff., 42, 44, 51 ff., 63, 64, 73, 87, 95,
96
Adiabene, 52
Aegean Sea, 25, 47, 61, 88
Agabus, 40
Agrippa II (Herod), 9
Alexander (brother of Rufus), 93
Alexander (coppersmith), 89
Alexandria, 16, 47, 51, 53, 55, 75,
79
Ananias (of Damascus), 11–14
Anatolia, 18, 19, 30
Andronicus, 83
Antioch (on Orontes), 16, 17, 18,
19, 20, 24, 40, 53, 58, 59, 64, 70,
74, 75, 93
Antioch (Pisidian), 19
Antiochus IV (of Commagene), 19
Antipas (Herod), 42

Apollos (Apollonius), 47, 51–57
Apostles, 18
Apphia, 83, 99
Aquila, 44–50, 82, 96, 97
Archippus, 83, 84
Aristarchus, 35, 76, 82, 98
Asch, S. 49
Asia (province) 47, 49, 66, 87, 94
Asia Minor, 25, 28, 31, 47, 76, 78
Asiarchs, 9, 49
Athens, 32

Baptism, 12, 53
Barnabas, 15–22, 30, 58, 73, 74, 75,
78, 80, 85, 93, 99
Barnard, L. W., 79
Barrett, C. K., 37, 65
Berenice, 9
Beroea, 27, 32, 96, 98
Bethlehem, 42
Black Sea, 47
Brown, R. E., 8

Bruce, F. F., 41, 59
Burkitt, F. C., 25, 60

Cadbury, H. J., 37, 38
Caesar, Gaius Julius, 97
Caesarea, 39, 82, 98
Canon (of New Testament), 70, 72
Captivity Epistles, 33
Cenchreae, 88
Cephas (see Peter)
Chrysostom (John), 95
Cilicia, 24
Circumcision, 31, 59, 60
Citizenship (Roman), 26
Claudius (emperor), 46, 78
Clement (of Alexandria), 95
Clement (of Philippi), 85
Colossae, 35, 66, 68, 71, 73, 82, 84,
    87, 99
Colossians, Epistle to, 29, 35, 66, 76,
    86
Commagene, 19
Corinth, 24, 27, 28, 32, 39, 45, 47,
    48, 60, 61, 62, 63, 88, 96, 97
Corinthians, Epistles to, 23, 32, 51, 54,
    55, 60, 61, 62, 63
Cranfield, C. E. B., 83
Crete, 57, 63
Cullmann, O., 8
Culpepper, R. A., 8
Cyprus, 17, 18, 21, 75, 99
Cyrene, 17, 93

Dalmatia, 63
Damascus, 11–14, 15, 92
Demas, 36, 86, 87
Derbe, 19, 98
Diary (in *Acts*), 38
Dio Cassius, 46
Disciples (at Ephesus), 53
Dives and Lazarus, 42
Doberus, 98
Dodd, C. H., 67, 79, 92
Drusilla, 9

Duncan, G. S., 41, 67
Dungan, D. L., 22
Edmundson, G., 78
Egnatian Way, 61
Egypt, 47, 51, 79
Ellis, E. E., 65, 90
Emmaus, 42
Epaphras, 36, 68, 82
Epaphroditus, 34, 84, 85
Ephesians, Epistle to, 87
Ephesus, 9, 32, 34, 44, 47, 48, 52,
    53, 54, 56, 67, 71, 82, 83, 89, 96,
    98
Erasmus, D., 95
Erastus (of Corinth), 88
Eunice, 30
Euodia, 39, 85, 94
Europe, 25, 61
Eusebius, 77, 79

Felix, 9
Festus, 9
Fortunatus, 56

Gaius (of Corinth), 97, 98
Gaius (of Derbe), 98
Galatia, 19, 30, 60
Galatians, Epistle to, 59, 60
Gallio, L. Junius, 9
Gentiles, 17, 20, 24, 40, 58, 64, 98,
    99
Gilchrist, J. M., 63
Glover, T. R., 81
God-fearers, 40, 94, 97
Goodspeed, E. J., 72
Gortyn, 64
Gould, S. B., 95
Grotius, H., 76

Haenchen, E., 38
Harnack, A., 46
Harrison, P. N., 90
Hatunsaray, 30
Hebrews, Epistle to, 34, 46, 57

Hellenists, 16, 53, 99
Hengel, M., 31
Hermes, 19
Hierapolis, 77, 82
Hobart, W. K., 37
Housman, L., 79

Iconium, 19, 30, 90
Ignatius (of Antioch), 70, 71
Italy, 63, 77, 82

Jailer (of Philippi), 95
James (the Just), 18, 20, 43, 93
Jason (of Thessalonica), 96, 99
Jerusalem, 15, 16, 17, 18, 24, 42, 43, 58, 62, 74, 78, 82, 87, 93, 98
Jerusalem, Church of, 24, 25, 98
Jerusalem, Council of, 20, 24, 30, 63
Jerusalem, Relief fund for, 39, 62–64, 87, 98
Jesus Justus, 35, 76, 86
Jews, 78
John (apostle), 5
John (the Baptist), 36, 41, 53
John Mark (see Mark)
Josephus, Flavius, 52
Judaea, 33, 53, 82, 96
Judas (of Damascus), 11, 12, 92
Judas (of Jerusalem), 24
Julius (centurion), 9
Junia, 83

Karaman, 19
Kavalla, 27, 31
Kerti Hüyük, 19
Knox, J., 72
Kraabel, A. T., 40

Laodicea, 66, 83, 84
Law of Athens, 69
Law of Israel, 69
Law of Rome, 69
Legg, J. D., 34

Lois, 30
Lucius, 35
Luke, 16, 20, 26, 27, 30, 31, 35–43, 44, 45, 52, 64, 82, 86, 94, 99, 100
Luke, Gospel of, 36, 37, 39
Luther, M., 57, 59, 74
Lycaonia, 30
Lycus valley, 68, 76, 82
Lydia, 94, 100
Lystra, 19, 26, 30, 32

Macedonia, 27, 32, 61, 82, 98
Makarios (archbishop), 21
Malta, 39
Manson, T. W., 60, 78
Mark, 18, 21, 35, 73–80, 82, 93, 100
Mary (Blessed Virgin), 42
Mary (of Jerusalem), 74, 93
Mary (of Rome), 89
Mediterranean Sea, 63, 78
Messiah, 48, 52, 54
Mitchison, N., 72
Mnason, 99

Nabataeans, 14
Neapolis, 27, 31
Neatby, W. B., 86
Nero (emperor), 78, 79
Nicolaus (of Antioch), 40

Onesimus (of Colossae), 66–72, 83, 89, 99
Onesimus (of Ephesus), 71, 72
Onesiphorus, 89
Orontes (river), 16, 19
Otranto (Straits of), 33

Paphos, 18, 76
Papias, 77
Pastoral Epistles, 9, 30, 34, 36, 63, 87, 89
Paul, 8, *et passim*
Paul, epistles of, 9, 43, 100
Perga, 75

Persis, 89, 100
Peter, 18, 43, 55, 75, 77, 80, 92, 93
Peter, First Epistle of, 28, 76
Pharisee and Tax-Collector, 42
Philemon, 67–72, 76, 83, 99
Philemon, Epistle to, 67, 76, 83
Philippi, 23, 26, 31, 32, 33, 38, 84,
  85, 94, 96
Philippians, Epistle to, 33, 39
Philo (of Alexandria), 55
Phoebe, 88, 100
Phrygia, 35, 66
Pontus, 47
Prisc(ill)a, 44–50, 82, 96, 97, 100
Priscilla, Cemetery of, 46
Prodigal son, 42
Prologues, Anti-Marcionite, 41, 77
Puteoli, 39

Quartus, 88

Ramsay, W. M., 82
Renan, E., 95
Roberts, C. H., 79
Robertson, J. A., 73, 77
Romans, Epistle to, 33, 48, 50, 63, 86,
  87, 88, 97, 98
Rome, 16, 39, 46, 48, 49, 50, 67, 75,
  78, 86, 89, 91, 93
Rufus, 93

St. John, P., 72
Samaritan, Good, 42
Secundus, 98
Selwyn, E. G., 28
Sergius Paullus, 9, 21
Silas/Silvanus, 23–28, 30, 31, 32,
  38, 45, 94
Simeon of Jerusalem, 42
Simeon Niger, 93
Simon of Cyrene, 93
Smith, J., 40
Smyrna, 71
So(si)pater, 45, 98
Souter, A., 64

Spirit (Holy), 53, 54
Stephanas, 56
Stephen, 16, 25, 53, 99
Stoney, J. B., 86
Suetonius, 46
Synagogues, 14, 31, 52, 94, 96, 97
Syntyche, 39, 85, 94
Syria, 24, 41, 48, 71, 96

Tarsus, 17, 93
Temple (Jerusalem), 98
Tertius, 87, 88
Theissen, G., 22
Theophilus, 40, 41
Thessalonians, Epistles to, 23, 28, 29,
  32
Thessalonica, 23, 27, 32, 82, 96, 98
Thyatira, 94
Tigris, 52
Timothy, 23, 24, 26, 29–34, 38, 60,
  68, 76, 82, 94, 98, 100
Titius Justus, 97
Titus, 39, 57, 58–65, 82, 100
Troas, 27, 31, 34, 38, 61
Trophimus, 98
Tryphaena, 89
Tryphosa, 89
Tychicus, 66, 69, 87, 98
Tyndale, W., 74

Urbanus, 86

Way, The, 48, 52, 53
'Western' text, 48, 51, 53, 54, 98
Wilcox, M., 40, 65
Wilson, S. G., 37
Wycliffe, J., 74

Yokefellow, 39, 85, 95

Zechariah (priest), 42
Zelophehad, 74
Zenas, 57
Zeus, 19
Zostera, 30